"*Girl, Arise!* challenges today's Catholic woman to embrace her moxie—her strength! Claire Swinarski's shoot-from-the-hip delivery employs scripture, the *Catechism*, and some pretty hefty saints to make a commonsense case for being Catholic and feminist in a culture that often misunderstands both."

Maria Morera Johnson
Author of *My Badass Book of Saints* and *Super Girls and Halos*

"It is abundantly clear that Claire Swinarski's ferocious young heart has fallen madly in love with Jesus and his messy, glorious, miraculous Church. If your feminine heart needs a jumpstart—or a shock treatment—*Girl, Arise!* will read as refining, often humorous, medicine."

Liz Kelly
Author of *Jesus Approaches*

"*Girl, Arise!* is a must-have guide for the woman searching for her place amidst Catholic teachings and real life. Claire Swinarski is the relatable, wise big sister we all need, calling forth the strength of women and a new generation of leaders in the Church."

Samantha Povlock
Founder and director of FemCatholic

"Whether you consider yourself a Pope Francis Catholic or a JPII Catholic, a pro-life Catholic or a social justice Catholic, or more of a Martha or a Mary, Claire Swinarski has a simple but compelling message in *Girl, Arise!*: You can (and should!) be a feminist, too."

Ashley McKinless
Associate editor at *America* and cohost of *Jesuitical*

"Smart, witty, and fearless. For Claire Swinarski, no hot-button topic is off limits. *Girl, Arise!* is filled with thought-provoking insights into questions Catholic women wish everyone were talking about. Finally we have a guide to navigating the modern world of Catholic feminism."

Lisa Cotter
Catholic speaker, podcaster, and coauthor of *Dating Detox*

girl, arise!

A Catholic Feminist's Invitation to
Live Boldly, Love Your Faith,
and Change the World

CLAIRE SWINARSKI

AVE MARIA PRESS AVE Notre Dame, Indiana

Founded in 1865, Ave Maria Press is a ministry of the United States Province of Holy Cross.

www.avemariapress.com

Paperback: ISBN-13 978-1-59471-893-9

E-book: ISBN-13 978-1-59471-894-6

Cover image © tomertu/Adobe Stock.

Cover and text design by Brianna Dombo.

Printed and bound in the United States of America.

Library of Congress Cataloging-in-Publication Data is available.

for Tess

Women of the entire universe, whether Christian or non-believing, you to whom life is entrusted at this grave moment in history: it is for you to save the peace of our world.

—Paul VI

Contents

Introduction

I am a Catholic feminist.

This causes a lot of confused looks and raised eyebrows, whispers and Instagram comments of "I don't think she knows what those words mean." It leads to a whole lot of not fitting in: Bible studies that want to focus on modesty and lipstick shades and social justice groups that want to pat my hand and remind me that my Church is backward and stupid.

But when I was in fifth grade and most kids were being brought to Disney World, my mom took my sister and me to Seneca Falls, New York, to see where the first women's rights convention had taken place. I remember standing there, learning about Susan B. Anthony, Elizabeth Cady Stanton, and Lucretia Mott, and feeling their spirit as strong as any Church sermon. Because of *course* everyone knows women should get paid as much as men, and of *course* we should end rape culture, and of *course* women can be strong, smart, and self-sufficient! My life as a starry-eyed feminist was born.

Then I went back to the real world and was slapped in the face with people saying *feminist* is a swear word.

Throughout my life I've met people from different parts of the country who act as though saying you're a feminist is equal to saying you want to swing naked on a wrecking ball Miley Cyrus–style. Being a feminist surely means you're a bra-burning, pro-choice crazy lady who believes cats are superior to humans and thinks men are simply sperm donors. Feminists are socialists, vegans, and Democrats, for heaven's sake! *And lo, she declared herself a feminist and there was a great clutching of pearls! Hide the children!*

But I'm a feminist for the same reason I'm honest, bold, and sometimes ragey.

Because Jesus was all of those things.

In a time when women were some of the lowest of the low, Jesus embraced them with open arms. He reached out and touched them, bringing them into his inner fold, trusting them with his wisdom and words. Think of Mary, the sister of Martha, sitting patiently at his feet while he taught instead of running around the house making dinner (see Luke 10:39). At the time, women learning from men was pure and utter insanity. By allowing women to sit and be educated he was radically breaking rules.

Or think of the moment when Jesus healed the crippled woman; he referred to her as "daughter of Abraham" (Lk 13:10–13, 16). This would have shocked those around him—never before had those words been spoken, only "son of Abraham." But Jesus says "daughter," reminding us that the arms of salvation are wide and welcoming of women. In effect, he's saying, *There's room for you here.*

Jesus reaches out to women many times throughout his ministry. When he saved the woman caught in adultery, he looked society's norms in the face and told them no (see John 8:1–11). He saw inherent value and dignity in this woman—in spite of her past, her sin, the mistakes she'd made and any mistakes thrust upon her. When he conversed with the Samaritan woman, an outcast getting water in the middle of the day, he gave her the greatest lesson of salvation history the world had ever seen (see John 4:7–26). When Jesus was resurrected, he chose Mary Magdalene to reveal himself to. Not Peter, or James, or John—a woman.

Catholic and *feminist* don't tend to go together, but I truly believe the Catholic Church is the most feminist institution in the world. To be a feminist is to believe that women are beautiful, unique, and equal in dignity to men. What other group believes women are made in the image of God? That we were commissioned by God himself? That women are capable of raising children in the direst of circumstances, no matter our income or relationship status?

Oh, yeah, and Pope John Paul II called us all geniuses.[1] Doesn't sound like woman-hating to me.

The Church is absolutely filled to the brim with examples of believing in the importance of womanhood. The world needs so much more than your impeccable cookie-baking skills or your ability to quote scripture from memory. It needs more than your hashtags. It needs the resilience, strength, and true beauty given to you by God.

Listen, y'all: I'm not meek and mild. I don't wait until I'm called on. I move fast and break things; I live with a fierce impatience and a spirit of *go, go, go*. I've never once in my life been called *ladylike*.

And I'm tired. I'm so, so tired of talking about whether leggings count as pants or if chapel veils are necessary. I'm tired of women's talks that remind me about the dangers of "the media" and the necessity of "guarding my heart." I'm tired of being reduced to a handful of physical attributes.

Oh, Catholic women. You sweet things. Come here. Let's shut our rule books; there will be time for all of that later. Put down that granola bar that tastes like sawdust. Let's go outside and get some fresh air, breathing in the Word of God and a spirit of truth. Let's stop finger-pointing and whispering about bathing suit choices. And please, for the love of all that is Jesus Christ, our Lord and Savior, let's stop saying that modest is hottest.

I want to sit across from you, hand you a steaming mug of coffee, look you in the eye, and tell you something:

It's up to us.

To quote the Venerable Fulton J. Sheen: "To a great extent the level of any civilization is the level of its womanhood. When a man loves a woman, he has to become worthy of her. The higher her virtue, the more noble her character, the more devoted she is to truth, justice, and goodness, the more a man has to aspire to be worthy of her. The history of civilization could actually be written in terms of the level of its women."[2]

If we spend our days discussing the perils of Facebook and that mean thing that political leader said, so will the rest of the world. If we spend our days racing toward holiness, helping our neighbors, and fighting for justice, *so will the rest of the world.* To be a Catholic feminist is to love the Church and to love our sisters, those next to us in the pew and those on the other side of the world.

I once eavesdropped on a men's talk. (I'm nosy. Let's establish that now.) The speaker referred to women as "teacups."

Oh, for the *love.*

I know what he was trying to say because he is a good man I know, love, and trust. He meant that men should be protectors, and that women's natural tendency toward being more relational leaves us greatly affected by our emotions. These are true sentiments! But can you imagine telling Mary, who stood by the Cross as her son perished, that she was a teacup? Or Joan of Arc, as she led men into battle? Or St. Teresa of Avila, as she became a Doctor of the Church? Teacups break when they're dropped. They crack easily. They have *floral patterns.* The women are the ones who remained at the Cross, witnessing tragedy. Women are crafted with fortitude and strength; the Holy Spirit has given us, too, a spirit of power and love and a sound mind.

Throughout my life I've had the chance to speak with amazing Catholic women who believe in their hearts and souls in the equal dignity of men and women. These women are founding nonprofit health centers, creating beautiful art, and healing from unspeakable wounds. They're fighting for peace, hope, and love, being bearers of the fruits of the Spirit. This—*this*—is what it means to be ladylike.

They're not teacups, and neither are you.

I see you, wondering why we get so lost in the trappings of what we look like and what we're supposed to be. I see you, sitting in women's talks, wondering why we're joking about shoes and reality TV when people are literally dying in the streets. (I love me some Kardashians, but come on now, there's *so much more* to talk about.) I see you wondering where the other Catholic women are when it comes time to protest racial injustices, hold the hands of post-abortive women, or care for the homeless. I see you listening as feminists tell you that you can't march, you can't write, you can't stand next to them in solidarity. They mock your beliefs in witty think pieces and memes, and both groups—the Catholic women and the feminists—shove you into boxes in which you don't belong. Bless 'em. I'm six feet two, y'all. I don't fit in many boxes.

There's room for you at this table. I'm scooting over. With this book, I want us to come together and discover the deeply rooted truth about Catholic womanhood. What does it mean to be a feminist? How can we support women in ways more meaningful than hot pink signs and hashtags? Is there a way to love margaritas and Mary and not be ashamed of either? Who are the biblical mothers we can look to when we need strength? How can we fully embrace the teachings of the Church while joining arms with our feminist sisters? By the time you're done reading, I want you to feel affirmed, confident, and encouraged in your journey as a Catholic woman.

It's time to embrace the *Catholic* and the *feminist*, blending them together to find God's true calling for you. It's time to find your own purpose and stop chasing that standard the world has so rudely dropped in your lap. There's room for you in this Church, sister, and there's room for you in this world. Promise.

Talitha koum.

Little girl, arise.

one

Claiming Room at the Table

What do you think of when you think of a "real Catholic woman"?

Let me paint you a picture of what I used to see.

I saw a woman who went to Mass every single day while raising her six impeccably groomed children. Her husband was a mechanical engineer, traffic control specialist, or one of those other jobs you can't really explain. She was quiet and submissive, letting her husband decide where the family lived and what they did on the weekends. She wore fashionable-yet-*modest* skirts and cooked organic, gluten-free dinners, all before leading her family in a Rosary—probably in Latin.

This idea of a "real Catholic woman" kind of haunted me because not only was I *not* that but I also didn't want to be. Six kids sounded like a lot. I don't wear many skirts. And the last time I was described as quiet was . . . never. I've literally never in my life been described as that.

So what's a girl to do? I sat through women's talk after women's talk that reminded me over and over again that the big problems facing me as a young Catholic woman were what I wore and how to treat men. These were the two doozies I was supposedly struggling with—according to speakers. But I really don't care how many inches long your skirt is, and I think how you treat a

1

man can't be summed up in an eight-slide PowerPoint presentation. Was there not a place for me in the Church? Was I not one of "us"?

I found myself feeling a touch isolated. More than once I've sat through presentations where I spent the whole time thinking, Seriously? The guys get to talk about being righteous warriors of justice while I have to have an hour-long conversation about whether leggings are pants? Are the guys getting lectured on how not to look at butts or . . . ?

As a bold woman who isn't afraid to raise her hand, I felt ignored by the Church in favor of girls who were quieter, more seen than heard. I wanted to dig my teeth in and talk about equal pay. Or refugees. Or systemic racism. Women could talk about abortion, sure, but not rape culture, subsidized childcare, or maternity leave laws. To me, those were "real Catholic women" issues. But everyone around me seemed to only want to talk about which brand of granola bar we should buy for the upcoming retreat snack. These experiences left me yearning to learn what a real Catholic woman was—and if I could ever hope to be one.

So what is a *real* Catholic woman? I could turn to other women, the media, or my priest of choice to investigate, but I went (almost) all the way to the top: the saints—one of my favorites, in fact.

According to Pope John Paul II, "The Church sees in the face of women the reflection of a beauty which mirrors the loftiest sentiments of which the human heart is capable: the self-offering totality of love; the strength that is capable of bearing the greatest sorrows; limitless fidelity and tireless devotion to work; the ability to combine penetrating intuition with words of support and encouragement."[1]

Let's unpack that. Pope John Paul II essentially offers four hallmarks of womanhood:

1. *Self-offering*. Women are meant to offer ourselves as gifts to the world. This could look like a thousand different things. God has different directions for each of us; we can't all follow the same road map. To cloistered nuns, a self-offering means giving up things such as NPR, football games, and outlet malls to spend their lives praying for others. To activists, a self-offering means spending long hours campaigning for justice. To stay-at-home moms, a self-offering means bypassing a career that could bless them in many ways in order to raise little saints. Many of us are somewhere in between.

2. *Strength in sorrow*. When tragedies occur, women often bring strength and steadiness to the situation. It's easy for us to paint women as emotional. I mean, who didn't cry during that rainy scene in *The Notebook*? Curse you, Ryan Gosling! But through the fresh soil of emotions, strength is planted like a seed and grows and grows. We're powered by our empathy and deep connection to others. If we were unaffected by events, we'd feel no desire to change them. Instead, we hear statistics about campus rape and feel compelled to try to make a difference. We see mass shootings on the news and feel a tug toward prayer and letter writing. We have a friend who has a miscarriage and we organize meal trains and spiritual bouquets.

3. *Tireless devotion to work*. The book of Proverbs tells us that a good woman "sets about her work vigorously; her arms are strong for her tasks" (31:17). Catholic women aren't afraid of work. We dig in our hands and get them dirty. Catholic women don't believe in sitting idle, waiting for the world to fix itself. We know that by raising children, starting businesses, voting, participating in the sacraments, and washing the dishes, we're serving the Lord.

4. *Penetrating intuition*. Ask a woman about her intuition and she'll most likely tell you a story about a time she knew not to go on a date with the guy who ended up being a jerk, or a time she felt compelled to show up to Mass ten minutes early

and encountered a friend sobbing and in need of consolation. According to a 2013 study, the neural connections in women's brains are more efficient than men's.[2] That means women are often good at interpreting social cues. Our "penetrating intuition" is a gift from the Lord; it allows us to see past what's on the surface and deep into the hearts of others. To quote the philosopher Edith Stein, "[Women] comprehend not merely with the intellect but also with the heart."[3]

Once I learned these markers of Catholic womanhood, my view of a "real Catholic woman" was greatly expanded beyond homeschooling and skirt length.

It suddenly included moxie.

For two years after college I was a campus missionary. I was every inch of the starry-eyed idealistic millennial you're envisioning. I'm *still* that, in many ways, but my time as a missionary challenged me in ways I could never imagine. One of those challenges? Meeting girls who were in that sticky in-between place of daily Mass and Gloria Steinem. Girls who showed up to large-group events and actually asked the speaker challenging questions? Girls who came to Bible study with confusion about why Jesus scolded Martha for getting crap *done*? Girls who listened to singer-songwriter Audrey Assad through their headphones while writing papers on feminist theory? Girls who organized trips to the soup kitchen on Monday, said their Rosary on Tuesday, and went to campus protests on Wednesday? Those were my *people*.

They had moxie.

What is *moxie*? According to good ol' Merriam-Webster, it's "energy, pep, courage, determination." It's hard to be a girl full of moxie in a world that pushes you toward being "meek and mild." Women ask for raises at work much less often than men.[4] Gender prejudices are instilled in us when we're only preschoolers.[5] The Bible itself has some confusing verses that can easily be misinterpreted as instructing women to zip their lips. The girls I met as a missionary were in the middle of the struggle between moxie and meekness.

But if you look up the word *meek*, it has two definitions. The first is "deficient in spirit and courage," which sounds, well, not ideal. But the second is "enduring injury with patience and without resentment."

What the heck, dictionary people! To me, those are complete opposites! To endure injury with patience brings to mind Jesus on the Cross, enduring the horror of horrors, all with patience and trust in the Lord. That takes an immense amount of spirit and courage. That second definition of meek—that's what I choose to identify with. A meekness that withstands. When Peter instructs us to have a "quiet and meek spirit" (1 Pt 3:4), I believe he's asking us to withstand enormous amounts of pain and suffering for the good of the Church, to not just sit idly while injustices take place around us and bite our tongues when we have something to say. To endure injury with determination is to live your life with a spirit of moxie. To have endless patience while discovering truth, picking up ideas and holding them up to the light? That, sister, is moxie. In that sense, meekness and moxie work perfectly twined together.

Think of the woman at the well. Jesus stands with her—an insane action at the time, by the way—and basically gives her a salvation history lesson. Instead of nodding and going, "Mmm hmm," what does she do? She questions him. She wrestles with what he's saying. After realizing that he's the Messiah, she returns to her village and tells everyone about him. On one hand, she was meek—she endured a lesson she didn't understand with great patience. On the other, she had moxie—she went out afterward and spread the Good News, no matter what it might cost her.

So who has moxie? Loud girls who lead marches and start petitions? Women at wells with whom Jesus decides to speak?

What if I told you that *all* Catholic women have moxie?

According to the *Catechism*, when we're baptized we're puri-
fied of our sins and also adopted as children of God. We become
"partaker[s] of the divine nature" and given "the power to live
and act under the prompting of the Holy Spirit" (*CCC*, 1265,
1266). So when we're baptized, we're given a role to play in the
world. That role isn't silent bystander, sister. It's to partake in the
Lord's divine plan. It's to live and *act* on God's will. It's to have
that moxie—energy, pep, courage, and determination—to fight
to break the shackles of a fear-based faith. That means that all
Catholic women have moxie, no matter what their Myers-Briggs
type is.

We butt heads when we want everyone to partake in divine
nature in the same way. We all have ideas about how women
should act in meetings or on retreats instead of desiring that each
woman find her own path through the Holy Spirit and act on
moxie in her own way. Because, of course, you can live out your
moxie by giving a testimony or starting a volunteer schedule at
your parish. You can also live out your moxie through prayer; by
asking God for huge, out-of-this-world miracles; or by waking
up at the crack of dawn to make coffee, fold laundry, and serve
others in a countercultural way. Is it so crazy to think that God
would bless us with a spirit of moxie and then ask us to use it in
different ways? I think not. I used to think moxie meant having
an opinion on every social issue and then loudly proclaiming
it from the rooftops. But I've come to realize that moxie simply
means bringing that spirit of courage and determination with
you wherever you go, whichever injustice you're encountering
in any particular moment. I stopped posting political Facebook
statuses about refugees and instead started donating clothes to
refugees. One is what people *think* moxie is. The other is what
moxie *actually* is. One opposes an attitude of meekness and servitude. The other works hand in hand with it.

Real Catholic women are full of moxie. Whether it's having
the courage to accept the Lord's call to the religious life, leaning

into your own determination to financially support your family, or having the immense amount of energy required to raise kids, our hearts beat with the gift of moxie. We aren't "Yes, sir" and "No, sir" women. We have a Lord who valued us so immensely he gave his life for us. How disrespectful would it be to spend that gift of life nodding silently and keeping our mouths shut?

There's no one way to be a "real Catholic woman," and we really need to stop pretending that there is. This enormous amount of pressure we put on ourselves to blend in and fit the mold has got to go. God, in his infinite wisdom, hasn't asked us all to be the same. How boring would that be? How dull of a world would it be if every morning we all woke up and led the exact same lives and had the exact same problems? Why is it such a big freaking deal if this woman homeschools her four kids, and this woman sends hers to a Spanish immersion school, and this woman sends hers to the Catholic school down the road? Why is it so insane that some women are called to spend eight hours a day in a cubicle and some are called to spend twenty-four hours a day in a convent? It's not. Because each of those women is living out her own unique call.

I'm able to learn something so beautiful from those women who live humble, steadfast lives. And I hope they're able to learn something from those of us who move fast and break things. We can *all* have spirits of moxie. We need women in the Church who are gentle and compassionate, and we need women in the Church who can cause a ruckus. We need women who are more comfortable in one-on-one settings and women who are public speakers. There's room at this table. Let's scoot over. The only way to understand where God is calling you specifically is to be in constant communication with him, asking him daily to guide you toward the path he's picked out for you.

So, a real Catholic woman? It has nothing to do with the number of kids you have. Or the type of swimsuit you wear. Or whether you rely on frozen meals two or three times a week. Or whether you prefer praise-and-worship music or some good ol'-fashioned Latin hymns.

By living with a spirit of moxie you're a real Catholic woman.

By demonstrating a true attitude of meekness you're a real Catholic woman.

By demonstrating a penetrating intuition you're a real Catholic woman.

By living out a tireless devotion to work you're a real Catholic woman.

By embracing strength in sorrow you're a real Catholic woman.

By constantly giving a self-offering you're a real Catholic woman.

By striving to see, know, and understand the face of Jesus you're a real Catholic woman.

two

Embracing the Beauty in Boldness

In early 2017 I was burned out at work, writing content for businesses about Facebook ad returns on investments and networking techniques after having spent two years working as a FOCUS missionary—work that I felt was moving the needle in the world. It's hard to go from spending your days talking about Christ and the meaning of life to walking business owners through the importance of search engine optimization. While I mostly enjoy my work and am incredibly thankful to be in the unique position of work-from-home mom, something was missing. I knew the importance of evangelization and discipleship but I wasn't living it out in any concrete way. I'd had to quit my Bible study because we moved to the suburbs and the drive during rush-hour traffic was unmanageable. I had plenty of people pouring into me at our new parish, but I wasn't pouring into others and didn't really see how to do so. I would see an article proclaiming that pro-life women couldn't be feminists and feel incredibly called to respond, but I had no real outlet to do so.

I was also just burned out on Catholics—Catholics fighting, Catholics complaining, and Catholics thinking they were Jesus flipping tables when really they were Pharisees barking orders. I was seeing the kind of conversations that don't include kind, openhearted, eager-to-learn discourse but instead consist of mudslinging and name calling. It seemed as if everyone was just rolling around in their own self-righteousness, so sure they were on the path to salvation while everyone else was on the prover- bial highway to hell. It was exhausting—I knew there were so many amazing people living out the works of mercy and bring- ing others closer to Christ, but I couldn't hear them over all the debates over the color of Starbucks cups.

I spent my second year as a FOCUS missionary at the Uni- versity of Missouri. My monthly drive from Mizzou to my home- town of Madison, Wisconsin, was about seven hours, and my music got old real fast. Audiobooks tend to make me sleepy, so I fell headfirst into the world of podcasts. I listened to all kinds of shows—true crime, business, news, book reviews, and more. But one genre that constantly let me down was that of the spiritual podcast. It seemed all the Catholic podcasts I encountered were a bit heady. They were knee-deep in the waters of theology and Latin. No offense to theology—plenty of women are deeply filled by talks of consubstantiation. But I was a journalism major in college, and my love of a good human interest story has always stuck with me. Instead of hearing statistics about Syria, I want to hear from a Syrian living in those statistics, you know? Instead of hearing about how the Early Church Fathers understood faith, I want to hear how faith influences women *today*. These spiritual podcasts were also mainly run by guys, who did a great job, but listening to them didn't feel like sitting around a campfire with your girlfriends and a glass of wine, which is the vibe I go for when listening to podcasts.

I started daydreaming that someone would start a podcast for Catholic women. I wanted one that would talk about real issues too—the kinds of topics so rarely covered in "women's talks." I even had a list in my mind of who would make great guests for this podcast, and I patiently waited for someone to start one.

Fast-forward two years. I was married with an almost one-year-old. I had been freelance content writing for a year, and although I'd been lucky to find a lot of success, I was starting to get the itch to do something with a little more *oomph*. I'd been writing website content for wedding photographers, and when one instructed me to write her "About" page as if it were, hand to heaven, "a love note from *Twilight*'s Bella to Edward," I just about screamed. I'd *had* it. As grateful as I was for the clients who were paying our bills, I had to find a creative outlet that filled my soul and let me wrestle with tough truths. There's a lot of honor in earning money to help your family put food on the table, but God had written a love letter on my heart: a love letter to women's rights, to intersectional feminism, to bringing women closer to his Son. And I felt as if I wasn't doing it in the slightest.

I was reading a biography on Dorothy Day titled *The World Will Be Saved by Beauty* when I was struck hard by a particular passage. Day, a Catholic and the cofounder of the Catholic Worker movement, was watching a march for the unemployed. It was the Great Depression and life was hard in a way I've never experienced. Day, who had been politically active for years picketing for women's rights and fighting for the rights of farmers, had recently converted to Catholicism. When she saw her radical friends marching, she had a question: Where are the Catholics?

That question started to haunt me because I think it rings true today. Where are the Catholics when it comes to sex trafficking? Where are the Catholics when it comes to immigration issues? Where are the Catholics when it comes to sexual harassment, equal pay, and rape culture?

I knew there were Catholics speaking out about these things, and I wanted to give them a platform. I'd had a blog for years, but I was pretty fed up with my own voice. I was writing for my day job, so just the thought of typing blog posts made my fingers hurt. But with a podcast I could go back to my journalism roots. I could interview women and tell their stories, and then use my skills as a marketer to share their words with the world. Where are the Catholics? I could find them. They weren't just in church buildings; they were in domestic violence shelters, state capitols, and nonprofits. They needed a microphone, and I had one.

Well, I didn't have one yet. But the internet could solve that problem before you could say "free two-day shipping."

Before my husband and I got married, we shared what we thought would be the hardest parts of marrying each other. After a moment of thought, I still remember him looking at me and saying, "I feel like one morning you might just wake up and say, 'God told me our family should go be missionaries in Guatemala for a year, so I bought our plane tickets and packed our bags. We leave tomorrow!'"

"Yeah," I said honestly. "I'd probably do something like that."

So I can't say he was too surprised when he came home from work and I told him my idea.

"That sounds awesome!" he encouraged me. Krzysztof (pronounced Kristoff—yes, like in *Frozen*) is nothing if not encouraging. He's a gold-medal encourager. If he didn't have arms like spaghetti noodles he would have made a great cheerleader in college.

"Are you thinking this fall?" he asked. "I'd have more time to help you with the tech side of things then." It was March.

"No . . ." I said carefully. "I built the website today. And reached out to a few women for interviews. And bought a logo. I'm thinking, like, next week."

We've all heard that when God closes a door, he opens a window.

I dove through that window as fast as I could.

Our family is big on Christmas movies. One of our all-time favorites is the original stop-motion *Rudolph the Red-Nosed Reindeer*, a 1960s production of clay figures and some not-so-po-litically-correct moments. There's a moment when poor Rudolph is lost out in the snowstorm; his mom wants to go look for him, but his dad barks in a deep voice, "No! This is *man's work*." My husband loves to repeat that sentiment—in his best imitation of Papa Reindeer—whenever I sheepishly hand him a stuck peanut butter jar or ask him to drop off our son at daycare. It's become something of a joke, turning "man's work" into whatever I'm asking him to do at any given moment. "Man's work" could mean getting me ice cream, taking our toddler to story time so I can write, or driving up north because I unfortunately fulfill the unfair stereotype of a woman who is a horrendous driver. It's a joke; it makes us laugh.

But within the Church, what is "man's work" versus "women's work"?

There's an undercurrent in Christian culture that seems to ask women to sit nicely and smile silently. Letting the menfolk handle the tricky problems of the world while we, like, iron their shirts or something. The men are the bold, the brave, the war-riors; the women pack the lunches. The men solve the problems; the women gossip. The men preach and teach; the women sit down and shut up.

Of course, it's not as if we go around *saying* those are our roles. But it's shown by our mainly male leadership boards and our mainly male politicians. There's no clearer demonstration than attending a men's talk, where they're instructed to defend the faith and rise up and lead, versus a women's talk, where we're reminded that our yoga pants are scandalizing. When we see women collaborating on an issue, people comment about how they really need to take some initiative and bring a man on who can just make *decisions*. But then people smile condescendingly and remind women how *beautiful* it is, their feminine genius—as long as that genius is used for things such as planning the pancake breakfast. Women's ministries—usually focused around mothering and party planning—are cutesy and cut off from the rest of the Church's work. Don't get me wrong—there are women who are greatly ministered to through women's ministry programs and who minister greatly through mothering and party planning. But in my experience, it's hard to find well-run women's ministries focusing on anything other than being a wife and mother.

I think some of this comes from the writings of Paul, the saint with whom Catholic feminists have a deep love/hate relationship. On the one hand, he can be a likeable guy. Former persecutor turned one of the world's greatest evangelists? An exceptional example of the deep, ever-flowing forgiveness of Christ? A sign that the Lord uses whom he wants, when he wants, and that we shouldn't judge others for their past sins? Check.

But he's also the writer of *those* passages, the ones we hear in Mass that make us squirm uncomfortably or roll our eyes. You know the ones.

1 Timothy 2:11–14: "A woman must receive instruction silently and under complete control. I do not permit a woman to teach or to have authority over a man. She must be quiet. For Adam was formed first, then Eve. Further, Adam was not deceived, but the woman was deceived and transgressed."

1 Corinthians 14:34–35: "Women should keep silent in the churches, for they are not allowed to speak, but should be subordinate, as the law says. But if they want to learn anything, they should ask their husbands at home. For it is improper for a woman to speak in the Church."

He seems like a stereotype of the most obnoxious Catholic guy we know, a typecast of toxic masculinity who reminds women to, well, sit down and shut up. Peter just seems so much more loveable. Or John. I mean, really, I'd probably take Job over Paul.

But I truly believe that Paul's words have been distorted, maligned, and misinterpreted.

Look at it this way: the Catholic Church clearly isn't afraid of making decisions that infuriate people. We claim that in the Eucharist, bread is literally transformed into Jesus' flesh—not exactly a popular idea. If the Church really thought women shouldn't be allowed to speak in church, the Church wouldn't let women speak in church. If the Church really thought women shouldn't be allowed to lead, we wouldn't have female Bible study leaders, administrators, or business managers. But we do. So please don't take my confusion about Paul's intentions as a railing against the Church. Clearly the Church doesn't take these phrases to mean "Be quiet, sit down, and keep your lips zipped." Some *members* of the Church certainly do, but not the Church itself. As Pope Benedict XVI said in a general audience in 2007,

> Nor was the female presence in the sphere of the primitive Church in any way secondary. . . . It is to St. Paul that we are indebted for a more ample documentation on the dignity and ecclesial role of women. He begins with the fundamental principle according to which for the baptized, "There is neither Jew nor Greek, there is neither slave nor free, there is neither male nor female; for you are all one in Christ Jesus." . . . The Apostle accepts as normal the fact that a woman can "prophesy" in the Christian community, that is, speak openly under the influence of the Spirit, as long as it is for the edification of the community and done in a dignified manner. . . . In short, without the generous contribution of many women, the history of Christianity would have developed very differently.[1]

So if you're diving into Paul's writings, do so knowing the truth: God loves women. The Church values women. Paul, in all his complications, affirms women, praises women, and fights for equality for women. He greets female missionaries. He thanks women for working for the Gospel. Paul speaks of love, compassion, and mercy; he speaks of a Father who goes above and beyond for every single one of his children. So there must be something deeper here.

Paul wrote to specific communities at specific times. Yes, there are truths that are never-ending, but some notes are clearly directed to the places he was writing to. And let us not forget that these communities were, in all likelihood, hot messes. The Church had *just* been formed. They didn't have encyclicals, Bible studies, and Bishop Barron's YouTube videos. They had word-of-mouth learnings and a handful of missionaries. So no judgment, but let's not pretend that these were necessarily the pinnacle of Catholic culture.

At the time of Paul's writing, women were second-class citizens, to say the least. They weren't allowed to learn from men, prophesy, or take part in ministry. So as Christian writer Sarah Bessey says, "Many scholars believe that in the exhilaration of their newfound freedom, a group of women were disrupting the meeting with questions and opinions, and Paul, as a reminder, asked them to learn in quietness and talk it over at home with their husbands. The gatherings weren't quite the place for this."[2]

Another school of thought suggests that Paul was trying to work within the culture of the people to whom he was writing. Yes, the early Christians were doing things radically countercultural, but they still needed to work within the context of their societies to effectively evangelize and minister. Paul warns the community of Corinth against speaking in tongues, something that the Church embraces as a gift of the Holy Spirit then and today. But at the time, he was most likely worried that the lack of order around prophesying and speaking in tongues would scare off newcomers. Paul wisely understood that women speaking in church—a place they previously hadn't even been allowed to be—may have the same effect. He states that this is "as the law says" (1 Cor 14:34), but the Old Testament never lists a law saying that women can't speak in church, meaning it's entirely possible that he was specifying a *local* law. Paul was trying to help the church in Corinth fit into the existing community. To quote Sarah Bessey again: "Paul's intention was to restore order to the community of God. And that order didn't include the silencing of all women any more than it included a blanket forever-and-ever prohibition on prophesying or speaking in tongues."[3]

This is all well and good, but in the Church, are women *truly* allowed to speak loudly and express our gifts? Should I have started a podcast, or should I have let a man teach instead?

Was leading other people to Christ *man's work*? Would a 1960s reindeer figurine pop up out of the blue to remind me so? Or worse, would a bunch of actual people do that? Are women truly supposed to sit quietly with our hands folded in our laps?

I find the answer to these questions best illustrated through a tale of two saints.

One was a young French girl born in the 1800s. She followed the paths of her older sisters straight into the convent, where she spent a few years doing a lot of praying, dish washing, and other less-than-glamorous tasks. When she died at the age of twenty-four, she hadn't accomplished anything remarkable. She wasn't beloved by thousands; she hadn't developed stigmata. She didn't see any bright white visions of Mary. To be honest, my own mother once asked me why Thérèse of Lisieux is a saint. She didn't, according to my mom, even *do* anything.

St. Thérèse is a Doctor of the Church.

The other is another French girl, born during the 1400s. After seeing visions of St. Margaret, St. Michael the Archangel, and St. Catherine of Alexandria, she went off to fight in the Hundred Years' War to pull France out from under England's thumb. She is the very definition of *fighter*. Joan of Arc got captured in 1430 and was *burned at the stake* at the age of nineteen.

She is upheld as an example of Catholic womanhood.

Thérèse and Joan couldn't be more different at first glance. Different missions, different calls, different ways of doing things. One lived inside a convent; one was a warrior. One had a seemingly incredibly dull life, and one had a dramatic, audacious life of sieges, battles, and bloodshed. One's biggest struggle before dying from tuberculosis was a deep annoyance at a nun who kept splashing her with dirty water on accident, and one fought on a battlefield.

But between these two saints, tied up in this tangle of holiness, lies one of the wonders of our faith.

God uses all types of people to do all types of things. He uses the quieter, introverted woman in service to others, folding laundry, making lunches, going over spreadsheets, or saying Rosaries decade by decade. He uses the louder, bolder woman out there on the battlefield. If the Church truly believed the only qualified women were quiet, subtle Thérèses, we wouldn't hold up boisterous, badass Joans as shining examples of womanhood as well. And vice versa.

Pope Francis writes,

> We should not grow discouraged before examples of holiness that appear unattainable. There are some testimonies that may prove helpful and inspiring, but that we are not meant to copy, for that could even lead us astray from the one specific path that the Lord has in mind for us. The important thing is that each believer discerns his or her own path, that they bring out the very best of themselves, the most personal gifts that God has placed in their hearts, rather than hopelessly trying to imitate something not meant for them. We are all called to be witnesses, but there are many actual ways of bearing witness.[4]

In other words, the Church has room for all types of people and all types of women. God's life is communicated to some women in one way and to others in another.

I'm a Thérèse-Joan combo, as I'm sure most of us are. There are days when prayer feels like the most essential work I can possibly do, and that God needs me on my knees more than he needs me out there freedom fighting. Other days I want to be at the forefront of things.

But when we're faced with that fed-up feeling that burned so deeply in my heart in early 2017, we have a few choices.

The first is to repress our feelings and just be generally grumpy and cynical toward the world.

The second is to take to the internet, airing our grievances and lashing out at those who disagree with us.

The third way is to actually do something.

But the third way is hard. It involves doing things such as researching local charities in your area that support refugees and actually purchasing things off of their Amazon wish lists. It involves picking up a book, not a Buzzfeed article, on a complex topic on which you want to become more informed. It involves voting, and anyone who has stood in line at a polling place with a toddler will tell you that, in the moment, democracy can feel overrated.

It involves something resembling a cross—and damn, that thing's heavy.

It sounds so novel, the idea of actually *doing* something. But I recently realized that dropping off a box of new baby clothes at our local Catholic Charities didn't just make me feel all warm and fuzzy; it moved the needle in some way that sharing a witty meme just can't. Doing something quietly without blasting it across the World Wide Web made me feel seen by the most important person: Jesus.

But I had this idea for a woman-focused web presence that just wouldn't stop nagging at my soul. I was thinking about the potential for a podcast with every freelance article and snack request and load of laundry. And so I could sit there, annoyed with Catholics, wondering when we'd get it together, or I could realize that I had money for a microphone, no fear of emailing total strangers and asking them to chat with me, and enough free time to launch a podcast.

So I did. On International Women's Day 2017, *The Catholic Feminist* podcast was born. Every week I chat with women about real heart topics: human trafficking, vocations, ethical shopping, abortion, infertility, racism, sexuality, and forgiveness. I'm able to ask hard questions and share women's stories with the world. Maybe I'm not a public speaker with an audience of millions, and I'm certainly not famous by any stretch of the imagination, but I have a skill set, and I can use it to bring glory to God and help fulfill his promises.

I don't sit down.

I don't shut up.

And I'm pretty sure St. Paul is happy about that.

three

Finding Freedom in Service

Growing up, Church to me meant mornings spent in uncomfortable pews, waiting not so patiently for post-Mass donuts, and wondering why other kids' moms let them bring books and toys to church. After getting yanked out of Catholic school and plopped into public, I suddenly had to start attending religious education classes (known in Catholic Land as Confraternity of Christian Doctrine, or CCD, where heathen public-school children such as myself are taught about Mary and the sacraments). Looking back, what I mostly remember is standing awkwardly around waiting for class to start, eating stale cookies at the end, listening to loud praise-and-worship music, and hoping TiVo wouldn't cut off the end of *American Idol*. But what I *really* remember was a series of DVDs we watched featuring Rob Bell, the former evangelical pastor. In one of the DVDs, he talked about how *Yahweh* sounds like breathing—inhale, exhale, inhale, exhale; that even as you sat across from someone saying "God doesn't exist," your breath would tell a different story, singing *Yahweh, Yahweh, Yahweh*.

I spent freshman year of college like many other college freshmen—memorizing the address on my fake ID and sleeping through Shakespeare classes. I never went to Mass, and each week was a different excuse—it was raining, I had to "study,"

Kourtney Kardashian was having her baby on the new episode of *Keeping Up with the Kardashians* airing that night (oh, how I wish that were a joke). I was free from CCD and a wood-paneled '70s-style church; I was free from Rob Bell. "Church teaching" was more of a suggestion, one of those nice things grown-ups tell you about but nobody actually *does*, like waiting until you're twenty-one to drink. I put people who thought hormonal birth control was harmful in the same group as flat-earthers. I honestly didn't know nuns still wore habits except at, like, a Renaissance fair or something.

But sophomore year slapped me in the face. In the span of three months I was denied entrance into my school's prestigious journalism program because of a horrendous GPA; a boy chewed up my heart, spat it on the ground, and stomped on it; and my grandmother passed away. So one Sunday morning I wandered around campus a little lost and a lot confused, and I somehow stumbled into the giant cinderblock building of St. Paul's University Catholic Center.

Today, if you go to Madison, Wisconsin, St. Paul's is stunning; it's everything a campus Catholic center would want to be, with saint murals, a gold-plated ceiling, and cozy rooms for discipleship. There's even a freaking *fireplace.*

But when I was a student there, it was a glorified bomb shelter made of concrete and leaking ceiling tiles. Barely any natural light came through the small series of paneled windows, giving it the feel of some kind of medieval dungeon. It felt about as far from Rome as could be. I once spent an entire discipleship session in that building figuring out who would take care of the dead bat in the corner.

I sat through that Mass by myself in the pew, my feet tucked up in front of me, chewing on the ends of my blonde ponytail. I couldn't tell you what the homily was about, but I can tell you I was wearing ripped jeans and was slightly hungover from a night of two-dollar shots at the Kollege Klub. I can tell you I felt as far away from God as a person could get. I was pretty sure, sitting in that Mass, that as a culture we had invented Jesus to get people to be nice to each other, the same way parents pretend that Elf on a Shelf is a sneaky mole for Santa Claus.

I don't remember the Gospel or the homily; I don't remember whether I got communion or what hymns were sung. But I remember the announcement at the end: that was the final day to sign up for winter retreat, the yearly off-campus gathering that took a hundred or so college students to a retreat center for talks, worship, and pizza.

After Mass I went into the office, staring at the stack of sign-up forms.

I wouldn't know a single soul.

And it was forty dollars.

And my atheist roommate was going to think I was super weird.

"Hey," a girl said, walking up to me. "Are you coming on the retreat?"

"I don't know. I'm not going to know anyone," I said, holding that sign-up form. "I'm not really a Church person."

"You'll know me," she said gently.

That girl was a FOCUS missionary. We exchanged names and numbers and she promised she would sit by me to avoid any awkward first-day-of-school lunchroom incidents. I laughed.

The first night on retreat was another praise-and-worship night, so similar but so different from my nights at CCD. All around me people were getting so *into* things, clearly feeling Jesus pulse through their veins. People threw their hands in the air and recklessly sang songs of praise, but I felt as if I couldn't breathe. It was as if the room had started to shrink. My vision went black and white. I left the room and sat on a bench outside, putting my head between my knees and taking deep breaths like you learn about in health class when you think you're about to pass out.

Another girl came up to me, having followed me out with a cup of water.

"I totally get it if you just want to be alone, but I saw you leave and I just wanted to see if you were okay," she said. That girl, just a student, is now a Dominican sister. I took the water from her and drank it gratefully.

"It's hot in there," I said, blaming my freak-out on a faulty air conditioning system. She just nodded and sat next to me, not offering words of wisdom or fortune-cookie kindness. She just sat there, in my presence, breathing.

Yahweh, Yahweh, Yahweh.

I didn't see Jesus or become infused with the Spirit that weekend. There were no stigmata occurrences. I didn't submit myself to the holy and apostolic Church or accept Jesus Christ as my personal Lord and Savior. But I met a couple women who turned into my nearest and dearest friends. One wasn't even Catholic at the time, although I would attend her baptism a year and a half later at Easter Vigil. The other I had actually met during Welcome Week, the first week of freshman year that's celebrated with tequila shots and thinking you're cool for attending frat parties. Those two women and I talked about everything from doubts and fears to the best place to buy jeans. No topic was too shallow or too deep; we could go from tide pool to ocean in a matter of minutes.

The Catholic Center became my home for the next two and a half years. That hideous bomb shelter wasn't just a stone building where you might get leaked on during a thunderstorm before the lights spontaneously flickered off. It was a place of the most authentic sisterhood I had ever known. It's where women questioned their faith; prayed on their knees; made brownies in the large, industrial kitchen for Newman Dinner; confessed sins; broke bread. When unfamiliar faces walked in, they were greeted. When unloved women flopped into chairs, they were loved. Bibles were studied, secrets were shared, promises were made. Sewn between scraps of a familiar liturgy was something completely unfamiliar to me—a sisterhood, and one that wanted me, flaws, questions, feminist rants, and all.

The community was far from perfect. More than once I heard low, judgmental grumblings of women who—*gasp*—had the audacity to wear tank tops to Mass. There was petty administrative drama between different leaders, as there will always be. But these women came alongside me, becoming some of my truest friends. They didn't shudder when I pointed out the lack of women's feet being washed at Holy Thursday Mass; they listened, thought, and offered their own opinions. We discussed heavy truths in a way that felt heartfelt and honest. It was basically the opposite of a social media experience.

And perhaps that's where *I* was served—not in the loud thumping of a praise-and-worship song with dramatic lights and a slideshow, not even through a casserole, but in being listened to and welcomed. In having people invite me into the conversation. In beautiful, broken women, incredibly ordinary, saying "I see you. I see you. I see you, and when I serve you, I serve Christ."

All men and women have been served by God, and we're all called to serve.

Genesis tells us that as Adam is called to serve the Garden, Eve is called to serve him as a companion (see Genesis 2:18). But we're so afraid of the word *serve*. We want to put it in a box and run away from it as fast as we can with our hands over our ears. *I'm called to more than that,* we think. This is understandable; for so long, service has been interpreted through the narrowest possible lens. And when women's service is only allowed to mean bringing the lemon bars to the parish picnic, those of us without aprons get feisty.

Our culture so grossly misinterprets the idea of service. We look down upon it and belittle it rather than respecting it as important and necessary work.

Mary is our ultimate example of service. When God asks her to become an unwed teenage mother, she humbly says yes—she gives her fiat and declares that she is the servant of the Lord (see Luke 1:38). She didn't know her service was going to entail riding a donkey while nine months pregnant and giving birth in a barn. She didn't know that her beloved son was going to be killed in the most brutal way possible. When Simeon later confronted her, grasping her hands and warning her that her soul would be pierced by a sword, she didn't sink away in fear. For Simeon also instructed her that the reason this would happen was so that "the thoughts of many hearts may be revealed" (Lk 2:35), and Mary, in what I'm sure was much human fear, understood.

Mary stood by Jesus through his tumultuous ministry, from his dust-covered birth to his bloody, horrendous death on the Cross. She stood and watched. We're so often tempted to paint Mary as a caricature of a sweet, mild-mannered lady in a blue cape. But the immense amount of strength Mary must have had in her servant heart to support Jesus throughout his ministry makes her one of the most robust, resilient characters in all of history. Mary had moxie of uncalculated levels.

She gave a whole lot more to the Church than lemon bars.

As Pope John Paul II says in his apostolic letter *Mulieris Dignitatem*, "From the first moment of her divine motherhood, of her union with the Son whom 'the Father sent into the world, that the world might be saved through him' (cf. Jn 3:17), *Mary takes her place within Christ's messianic service*. It is precisely this service which constitutes the very foundation of that Kingdom in which 'to serve . . . means to reign.' Christ, the 'Servant of the Lord,' will show all people the royal dignity of service, the dignity which is joined in the closest possible way to the vocation of every person."[1]

When women are called to serve, we're called to take part in salvation history. We're called to be like Jesus, who "did not come to be served, but to serve, and to give his life as a ransom for many" (Mt 20:28). If you don't want to serve, you don't want to be like Jesus.

So, yes, women are called to serve. But there are many, many ways to be of service.

You can serve your family by cooking dinner.

You can serve your classmates by showing up to group project meetings on time.

You can serve your patients by using your skills as a surgeon to fix limbs, bones, and hearts.

You can serve your community by running a domestic violence shelter.

The problem isn't *service*—it's how little value we give to service.

By being called to serve, we're called to a mission as high as a person can be called: to be like Christ. And what's a life without service?

As Martin Luther King Jr. said, "Everybody can be great, because everybody can serve. You don't have to have a college degree to serve. You don't have to make your subject and your verb agree to serve. You don't have to know about Plato and Aristotle to serve. . . . You only need a heart full of grace, a soul generated by love."[2]

As women, we're called to serve everyone around us. But there's one group in particular that we must put before all others.

The *Catechism of the Catholic Church* states,

> The duty of making oneself a neighbor to others and actively serving them becomes even more urgent when it involves the disadvantaged, in whatever area this may be. "As you did it to one of the least of these my brethren, you did it to me." This same duty extends to those who think or act differently from us.

The teaching of Christ goes so far as to require the
forgiveness of offenses. He extends the command-
ment of love, which is that of the New Law, to all
enemies. (*CCC*, 1932–1933)

We have a special call to serve the disadvantaged, the
marginalized.

We can serve the disadvantaged by refusing to buy clothes
made with slave labor, even when those clothes are discounted
75 percent, or by giving more than the old cans at the back of
our pantry to the soup kitchen. We can serve by actually *doing*,
actually giving or showing up, not just posting a witty think
piece on Facebook.

Man, it would be easy to not care, wouldn't it? To shop wherever we wanted, do whatever we wanted, and vote in a way that
benefits only us—our towns and our lives. It would be so beau-
tifully easy to read about new laws passed and not think of the
people they will affect or the families they will rip apart. Just as
it would have been easy, I imagine, for St. Joan of Arc to pretend
her visions were just dreams, St. Gianna Molla to just get that
advised abortion, or mama Mary to say, "You know, Gabriel, that
sounds great, but I think I'm good with the life I've got."

But our faith isn't one of prosperity gospels and feel-good
kumbaya songs. It's a faith of the Cross, of someone who came to
serve instead of to be served. If you want something easy, you're
looking in the wrong place. And just because the people you're
serving are ungrateful, jerks, or—*gasp*—pro-choice, doesn't
mean you're not still called to serve them with love.

We all have saints who seem to follow us around, whispering
in our ears and tugging on our hands when we aren't sure where
to go. Although I have a small tribe of them, nearest and dearest
to my heart is St. Teresa of Calcutta, one of the greatest examples
of might, mercy, and moxie I think the world has ever known.
What if Mother Teresa had decided that she was just too busy/
frustrated/insert-complaint-here to care about the poor? She

would have never founded the Missionaries of Charity, which serves the poorest of the poor and cares for the sick and dying in their last moments.

Mother Teresa served a large number of poor, sick, and orphaned Indians, but she also constantly served the sisters she worked with. When I interviewed Mother Mary Catherine, a former Missionary of Charity, for my podcast, she said it wouldn't be surprising to walk by and see Mother Teresa cleaning out a toilet at the motherhouse. Mother Teresa knew that it wasn't about how many people you served but how many ounces of love you were able to pour into every act of service. As she said, "I do not agree with the big way of doing things. To us, what matters is an individual."[3]

To serve doesn't necessarily mean hopping on an airplane to Guatemala and becoming a missionary. But it does mean caring. So, no, it doesn't feel as if I'm changing the Church when I bring lemon bars. It doesn't feel as if I'm making a difference when I wash my son's sticky, peanut-butter-covered fingers again. It doesn't seem earth-shattering when I'm writing for the parish newsletter, recording podcast interviews, or sending sponsor invoices.

And so when thinking about service, I issue three challenges. The first is that you reconsider what it means to serve, remembering that to serve is to be like Christ. The second is that you don't run away from serving, keeping close to your heart the fact that our duty is to serve all of humanity. And the third is that you recognize the service you're already performing, embracing the fact that, as Mother Teresa said, "Love begins at home, and it is not how much we do, but how much love we put in the action that we do."[4]

Catholic women, we need to act as Christ's presence on earth, and we can't do that if we're afraid of a five-letter word.

> Christ has no body but yours,
> No hands, no feet on earth but yours,

Yours are the eyes with which he looks
Compassion on this world,
Yours are the feet with which he walks to do good,
Yours are the hands, with which he blesses all the
    world.
Yours are the hands, yours are the feet,
Yours are the eyes, you are his body.
Christ has no body now but yours,
No hands, no feet on earth but yours,
Yours are the eyes with which he looks
compassion on this world.
Christ has no body now on earth but yours.

                                        —St. Teresa of Avila

four

Being Called as a Leader

I've always been bossy. I haven't always been a leader.

I used to have a fear of leading, to be honest. Oh, sure, I can make some decisions. I can point us in the right direction, probably. But after I met Jesus in college, I questioned so many things about who I was and what the world wanted from me. I'd done so much stupid crap and said so many hurtful things—surely Jesus would never use me to lead others.

The first time someone called me a "thought leader" because of the sudden popularity of the podcast, I kind of wanted to barf. I didn't want people to think I had it all together or hold me up as some pinnacle of Catholic womanhood. To put it bluntly, I had no interest in becoming Catholic-famous; the part of me that had always felt a little left out and a little left behind since middle school gave me an automatic resentment toward the "in" crowd. Let those women lead. I would be in the back banging the drum, serving the coffee, and rabble-rousing.

I think my view of Catholic leadership was just as screwed up as the world's view of service. I thought leaders had it figured out, as if the answers to life's big questions could be found in a Google search and stuffed into your back pocket. Leaders didn't question. Leaders didn't doubt. Leaders would never sit in Mass and wonder if Jesus' life and death and everything else we proclaim to believe all really happened or if they're just a story we made up to make ourselves feel better about our smallness. Leaders swallowed Church teachings as easy as sugar, knew exactly who to vote for, and had a scripture-certified answer to every single question.

Leaders in the world? Those were ice queens—tough as nails; they wore pencil skirts and stiletto heels and had crow's feet, I was sure of it. I certainly fit in better with that group than with the Nice Church Ladies, but that didn't feel quite right either. Those women had to fight tooth and nail for every promotion; after all, they make up only 25 percent of executive- and senior-level officials and managers, hold only 20 percent of board seats, and are only 6 percent of CEOs.[1] The women that made it to the top had to make immense sacrifices I wasn't sure I wanted to make. Leaders in that realm, I was sure, didn't have time to be soccer moms or classroom volunteers. They were "above it." But I deeply wanted to be.

So I didn't want to serve. But I couldn't lead. Where would I end up, exactly?

Being exactly what I was called to be, what we're *all* called to be in some capacity: a servant leader, made in the image of God.

I know some listeners of the podcast see me as some type of spiritual leader. And I suppose in some ways I am. I'm not afraid to bring issues to the forefront or to take a stand when one needs to be taken. Heaven knows I excel at planting a stake in the ground. But I also hope I'm the type of leader who will hold up teaching to the light and see if it can withstand the Word. I want to be a leader who leads others to truth, not to popular opinion or neat-and-tidy answers. I know I'm the leader who can drop some witty wording, send some emails, and wrestle a toddler through a diaper change, but I also want to be a leader who helps change the world, as big and outrageous as it sounds.

We think of *serving* as the opposite of *leadership*, but that's only because we don't understand either term the way God does.

When it comes to women in leadership roles, I laugh at those who would dare say women haven't been breathed into by the same Spirit who grants men leadership qualities. The Bible is full of women who weren't afraid to lead.

Start with the book of Exodus. When I was growing up, one of my favorite movies was *The Prince of Egypt*, the classic '90s animated film featuring the guy who later played Voldemort as the evil Pharaoh and poor, sweet Moses trying to lead his people out of slavery. I mean, nothing says "children's movie" like brutal beatings and a dead Egyptian army, am I right? Then and now, I love Miriam, Moses's sister.

Miriam was tough, strong, and incredibly faithful, reminding Moses at his weakest points that God hadn't abandoned him. Now, I'm guessing Miriam didn't actually sound like Sandra Bullock, but she really was a rock star. Homegirl saves her brother's life by sending him down the Nile and then helps the Israelites find water while wandering the desert for forty years. Miriam has a two-line song in Exodus (15:21) that's also considered to be some of the oldest words in the Hebrew Scriptures. So, just to clarify, *some of the oldest known words in the Bible* are spoken by a woman.

Follow Exodus with the book of Judges, an underrated book that teaches us to watch out for women wielding sharp objects. Deborah, a female general and prophetess, has predicted that the enemy will be conquered by a woman. The Israelites win the battle, the enemy general is fleeing, and Jael convinces him to come into her tent so she can give him refreshment and a place to rest. He falls asleep and she drives a tent peg into his head. Whoa. Deborah sings that Jael is "blessed among women" for crushing the enemy (Jgs 5:24). Where else do we hear that phrase? When it's repeated to Mary, that she is *blessed among women* for crushing the ultimate enemy by bearing the Son of God (see Luke 1:42).

Protestants don't have the book of Judith, and they're missing out because she's amazing. Judith's city is surrounded by the enemy during a time of war, and they're all basically about to wave the white flag and give up. Understandable, since everyone's starving to death. But Judith asks for a chance to sort things out. She sneaks out at night with a bag of cheese and wine and flirts with the evil general until he agrees to speak with her. She gives him the snacks she brought until he gets all drunk and sleepy, and then she casually chops off his head. Talk about getting it *done*. What did I say about women and sharp objects in the Bible?

Or take Vashti, in the book of Esther. Vashti was a beautiful Persian princess who married a king. One night, when she and her husband were having two grand feasts, one for men and one for women, he had a *bit* too much to drink and demanded that she come to the men's feast and parade around, showing off her beauty. (Some translations have him demanding her to wear only her crown. Uh, yikes.) Vashti wasn't into being seen as some sexual piece of meat, so she declined the oh-too-kind offer. She serves as a beautiful example of how God comes before all—even our husbands. If your husband asks you to do something that isn't in line with God and his kingdom, then declining is the holy thing to do. Too bad Vashti was a bit before her time and her refusal got her divorced and exiled. But I love Vashti because she demonstrates the power of womanhood. Yes, we're beautiful. No, we're not beautiful *for you*. We have the right to say yes and no and anything in between when it comes to our bodies. Vashti lost her life of luxury by standing up for herself—sounds pretty feminist to me.

This king is seriously bad news, y'all. After Vashti, he picks up Esther in some complicated, biblical-times version of *The Bachelor*. Esther is a Jew, but she keeps her heritage a secret. When the king gives permission for the killing of all the Jews, Esther steps up to the plate and saves her people by diplomatically convincing her husband to spare their lives. This took immense courage—not only was it unheard of for a woman to stand up to her husband in such a fashion, but this king had already proven he wasn't about to tolerate uppity wives. Esther used her gifts to find a diplomatic solution and save God's Chosen People; she wasn't going to just sit aside while her husband made careless decisions that would destroy lives.

Or what about seeing Mary, meek and mild, as a feminist leader? Mary is offered a huge choice from God, possibly the craziest task of anyone, save for Jesus, and continues to say yes. Mary has to live within the customs of her time—when an unmarried pregnant woman could be stoned—and chooses to give birth to the Son of God. Anyone she might have told probably thought she was nuts, but not her cousin Elizabeth, who reminded her she was "blessed among women" (Lk 1:42). (There it is again!) Mary then has to ride a donkey for miles while nine months pregnant, give birth in a stable, and then raise the Son of God. She's living out her true feminine nature by making enormous, life-altering sacrifices for her family, making her the ultimate feminist.

So blessed are *you* among women for valuing these spiritual mothers who have come before us. These *leaders*. Serving. Leading. They're opposite sides of the same heavenly coin we're all reaching for. They're both vital to the Body of Christ.

I spent two years as a college missionary. During that time I got into two separate heated conversations with men about whether or not women could lead teams of missionaries. Besides their gross misinterpretation of Paul, what deeply infuriated me about these men's lack of understanding was that they were unable to comprehend that leadership doesn't have to look one particular way.

We often think that to *lead* means to have power and dominance, that leading simply means being in charge of a group of people and having the loudest voice. But Christ shows us true leadership—a leadership that's gentle and servant-hearted, a leadership that often looks more feminine—again and again.

So the world needs women as CEOs, heads of state, and school principals. The world needs women who will lead the PTA and the Girl Scout troop, who will stand in front during protests and knock on doors. You can't simultaneously claim that men and women are fundamentally different and that having so few women in traditional leadership roles doesn't matter. Either women bring something special to the table or we're all exactly same.

The world also needs women to lead the Church, although again, this may not look how some would expect it to.

One of the biggest shots that can be taken at the Catholic Church is its lack of female leadership. Male priests, male bishops, male cardinals, and a male pope—nary a woman in sight. It was a sticking point for me, one facet of the Church I just couldn't swallow. After all, if we're called to serve, why wouldn't our service be accepted in what seems like the only important leadership positions?

But here's an important truth: being in charge isn't the only way to lead. Consecrating the Eucharist, although one of the most important aspects of our faith, isn't the only way you can serve a parish or faith community.

I could list a thousand talking points about why women aren't admitted to the priesthood, but for every one I'm sure you could come back with a zippy response about why that's stupid. If I mention that Jesus handing Peter the keys to the kingdom founded the Church (see Matthew 16:18–19), and that every pope has been a successor of Peter and therefore we have to trust the Church as a kind and loving parent instead of one that wants to keep us down, you'd probably point to the Crusades or sex scandals with raised eyebrows. If I say that the Church in her wisdom decided to have men as our pastors due to their masculine complementarity to the feminine nature of the Church, you surely would remind me that women could give great homilies, could be great shepherds, could drop some wisdom nuggets in Confession. That's all true.

And yet . . .

Aren't there a million and one ways for women to serve the Church? What if instead of focusing on what we can't do, we started focusing on what we can do? How many of us try to bring a woman's voice to the table—running for pastoral council, volunteering to lead a ministry service, or becoming certified as a spiritual director? Or do we run the other way, angry at an institution we see as denying us equality, refusing to participate in areas where we could flourish?

St. Catherine of Siena said that if we are what we're meant to be, we will set the world ablaze.[2] In the 1300s, she courageously visited Pope Gregory XI and spent three months begging him to move the papacy back to Rome, instead of France, where it had been relocated in a fit of political drama years prior. When he finally did and was then consumed with second thoughts, this illiterate Doctor of the Church basically scolded him: "I beg of you, on behalf of Christ crucified, that you be not a timorous child but manly. Open your mouth and swallow down the bitter for the sweet."[3]

Was she the pope? No. Did she take actions that altered the entire future of the Catholic Church? Yes. Did she remind a flipping pope to be *manly*?! I mean, for the *love*. Talk about servant leadership in a bold manner. Church history is full of the richness of women leadership. We jump out from every page—speaking, guiding, praying, serving, and leading. We're woven into stories, rituals, and creeds. We're an active part of the living, breathing Body of Christ.

Dominican Fr. Wojciech Giertych has served as the theologian of the pontifical household for both Pope Francis and Pope Benedict XVI. He's pretty much the guy to go to with Catholic questions. When asked by Catholic News Service about why women are unable to hold the position of priest, he said, "In theology, we base ourselves not on human expectations, but we base ourselves on the revealed word of God. We're not free to invent the priesthood according to our own customs, according to our own expectations. Christ was courageous with respect to the local social customs, he was not afraid to be countercultural. He didn't follow the expectations of the powerful, of Pilate, of Herod. He had his own work, his own mission."[4]

Fr. Giertych goes on to say that theologians simply can't know why Jesus did everything he did. We can't say why he chose only men as his apostles. Believe you me, it may be one of the first questions I ask him when I get to heaven. But he did.

I'm not saying to stop questioning. Oh, sister, I would never say such a thing. Questioning clarifies our faith; it brightens our spirit and points us to heaven. The very meaning of *Israel* is "to wrestle with God," and wrestle I do. I'm asking you to love the Church. I'm asking you to love her through your confusion, misunderstandings, and hurt. I'm asking you to shake like dust from your feet what you previously thought about equality and understand that, to quote Pope John Paul II, "women will increasingly play a part in the solution of the serious problems of the future: leisure time, the quality of life, migration, social services, euthanasia, drugs, health care, the ecology, etc. In all these areas a greater presence of women in society will prove most valuable, for it will help to manifest the contradictions present when society is organized solely according to the criteria of efficiency and productivity, and it will force systems to be redesigned in a way which favors the processes of humanization which mark the 'civilization of love.'"[5]

As feminists, we can't let anger, frustration, or jealousy hold us back from helping people throughout the world.

So although having women in conventional leadership roles is important, it's about much more than leading Fortune 500 companies. It's even about more than leading a homeschool co-op. It's about leading a culture closer to Christ, closer to the truth of all that is. It's about holding up a finger that points at corrupted power, discriminatory practices, and slave labor, and says "Not on our watch." It's about using traits typically considered "feminine"—graciousness, hospitality, generosity—to improve a world that so often spits on these traits. As Pope Francis recently wrote, "Indeed, in times when women tended to be most ignored or overlooked, the Holy Spirit raised up saints whose attractiveness produced new spiritual vigor and important reforms in the Church. We can mention St. Hildegard of Bingen, St. Bridget, St. Catherine of Siena, St. Teresa of Avila, and St. Thérèse of Lisieux. But I think too of all those unknown or forgotten women who, each in her own way, sustained and transformed families and communities by the power of their witness."[6] We, too, are called to transform our communities with the power of our witness.

When Jesus meets with the Samaritan woman at the well (Jn 4:4–26), he is breaking about eight thousand rules. Like, it's absurd how insane his talking to her would have seemed. He basically gave that woman a Bible study in a few short sentences: he explained who he was and what he meant, and he allowed her to question and hold up his story to the light. When she decided he was, in fact, telling the truth, what did she do?

She told many. She spread his name. She accepted her role as a leader, as someone with *something to say*. She didn't "Aw, shucks" her way out of it; she didn't allow others to dictate her role in the world. She ran after Christ, arms wide open, proclaiming the Gospel from the rooftops, living the truth.

So, yes. I'm bossy. I like to be in charge and make the decisions. And a few thousand women listen to me through their headphones every week. But that still isn't what makes me a leader. What makes me a *leader* is that I'm able to use my heart and intellect to make holy, noble decisions as often as I can and point others in the same direction. As a leader, I can sit with women who are in the murky muddiness of spiritual confusion and honestly say "I've been there. Here's how I got out. Here's where I am now. I'm with you."

five

Becoming Pro-Life and Pro-Women

After I left FOCUS I was fumbling a bit career-wise. I had a short stint as a marketing assistant that left me feeling as if the cubicle life was not the life for me. The well-meaning advice I was often given frustrated me: *You just need to find what you love to do.*

I mean . . . I loved reading. I loved writing. I loved chips and salsa. I loved Pinterest. I loved Jesus. I loved blog-stalking. There didn't really seem to be a clear career path there.

Then I had my millennial moment: I decided to freelance. I had a few very, very helpful friends who walked me through how to get freelance writing gigs. Freelance writing seemed to be the wave of the future: as businesses and publications faced shrinking budgets, they needed to bring on writers to whom they owed no health insurance or retirement plans. Quick, easy articles followed by checks in the mail: it seemed sustainable if you were a hustler and knew how to pitch. I was both of those things.

Eventually I transitioned into mainly helping businesses with web copy and content marketing, but I spent a solid year making a pretty decent income writing one-off articles and blog posts. When I was contracted by Vox.com to write a piece on being a pro-life feminist, it felt like a major win: the paycheck was solid, the topic was something I was passionate about, and Vox has a huge readership.

Oh, sweet, sweet Claire. Naïve as the day is long.

The emails began pouring in the next day. Although many of them were angry and full of vitriol—Vox didn't have an open comments section, meaning that people had nowhere to send their anger except straight to my poor, burdened email account—I wasn't offended in the least. I've been blessed with a pretty thick skin when it comes to feedback on my writing, and I knew that the topic was going to be unpopular. But I *was* fascinated by how many emails told me not that abortion was right but that I couldn't possibly be a pro-life feminist—those two things simply could not, would not, coexist.

This continues to be something I hear at least once a week, whether through email or Facebook comments: Pro-life feminists are unicorns—nice to think about but not actually romping through the forest. Feminists *have* to be for "my body, my choice." If you don't believe Planned Parenthood is God's gift to womanhood, you're anti-choice, anti-women, and anti-humanity in general.

So where does that leave a woman like me?

Let's put something out on the table right here, right now: there's one huge issue that divides secular and Catholic feminists.

We can (for the most part) get on the same page about so much. Equal pay? No-brainer. Ending a culture of rape and harassment? Of course we support that.

But pro-life issues seemingly will forever be that hefty orange caution tape that divides us.

To me, this isn't just an issue that causes finger-pointing and hurt feelings. It's more than that. This is where the Church opens wide her arms, steps it up, and shouts "We're pro-women" in her loudest voice.

If only people would *listen.*

Like so many other things, there are extremes on both sides of this issue that are hurtful and unhelpful. On one end of the spectrum, you have secular feminists who insist that pro-life women are ignoring bodily autonomy; that we want to create baby-making machines and we only view women as uteruses. They believe if you ever utter a word against a woman's right to make choices about her own body you're an anti-women redneck who needs to go read some Gloria Steinem. On the other end, you have pro-life advocates who are really more pro-birth—they're anti-abortion but would like to remind you that sex leads to babies, you should have thought of this beforehand, and honestly, this is what you get. Oh, and after you go through a tumultuous nine months and actually bring a child into this world, you get no help or hugs from them.

Not only are neither of those extremes helpful, kind, or loving in the slightest but also neither speaks the *truth.*

Abortion is wrong—not simply because it ends a life but also because it isn't good for women.

The idea that abortion is undesirable is an idea most of us can probably wrap our heads around. The Church has been against abortion from the beginning; the *Catechism* clearly states that "human life must be respected and protected absolutely from the moment of conception. From the first moment of his existence, a human being must be recognized as having the rights of a person—among which is the inviolable right of every innocent being to life" (*CCC*, 2270). Scientists will argue about when life begins—When there's brain activity? A heartbeat? Toenails?— but there's no scientific black-and-white answer. As Catholics we can confidently say that life begins at conception. However, even if you aren't Catholic or Christian at all, it's pretty obvious that there's a significant difference between a baby the day it's conceived and a baby on the day it's born. Somewhere along the line, *life* begins, and there's no scientific method that allows us to decide that fact in a laboratory. So erring on the side of *not* ending a life seems to be the most rational, moral, loving conclusion, even if you take out of the picture such Bible verses as "Before I formed you in the womb I knew you" (Jer 1:5).

But like so many teachings, something that seems simple and straightforward within a nice little book becomes a thousand shades of complicated when you're staring a terrified, pregnant, broke-as-a-joke college student in the eye.

According to the Guttmacher Institute, a pro-choice think tank, "The reasons patients gave for having an abortion underscored their understanding of the responsibilities of parenthood and family life. The three most common reasons—each cited by three-fourths of patients—were concern for or responsibility to other individuals; the inability to afford raising a child; and the belief that having a baby would interfere with work, school, or the ability to care for dependents. Half said they did not want to be a single parent or were having problems with their husband or partner."[1]

To break it down, women mainly have abortions due to a *lack* of choice. Whether it's a lack of finances, career opportunity, or a stable partner, a woman is more likely to choose abortion as a reaction to something lacking in her life. This isn't an empowering decision. This is a decision made out of fear. This isn't "my body, my choice" but rather "I feel I have no other choice."

That same study specifically says that 75 percent of women who obtain abortions are poor or low-income.[2] To anyone who says that they can't imagine why a woman would choose an abortion, I suggest imagining being pregnant with no money to pay for ultrasounds or diapers. This is quite a bit beyond not being able to afford the boutique bedsheets over the mass-market ones. This is a true reckoning that you may not be able to afford the bare necessities for your child.

Abortion is consistently seen as the solution to these problems. A woman can't afford a baby, can't get ahead in her career, can't imagine being a single mother: enter abortion, a one-size-fits-all solution that can take away her worries.

But what if instead of providing someone pills, a procedure, or a surgery that ends a life, we took that energy and used it to make the world a friendlier, more welcoming place for mothers?

We also forget here in our cozy United States bubble that in many parts of the world, baby girls aren't seen as little Instagram models for our matching headbands. Gendercide is real. *Petals in the Dust* is a documentary showcasing its effects on India, where girls are seen as less desirable to a family culturally and are often aborted. There's an old Indian saying that "raising a girl is like watering another family's garden." Girls are seen as something to be given away, either to the trash or to another family, not as people to be valued and upheld. In the book *Unnatural Selection: Choosing Boys Over Girls, and the Consequences of a World Full of Men*, author Mara Hvistendahl argues that most "missing females" in the world, causing such skewed gender statistics in primarily Asian countries, are killed by second-trimester abortions.[3] So while secular feminists may shout a rallying cry of pro-women, pro-choice, the fact is that the very operation they celebrate is used across the globe to literally kill off our own gender.

It's not good for women to be in states of mortal sin. It isn't beneficial to their hearts to allow them to end lives. It's nonsensical to claim that you're against abortion but don't want to limit others' options: What if we said the same about animal abuse, heroin addiction, or drunk driving? Wrongs are wrong, and harms harm, and the truth, as the American novelist Flannery O'Connor once said, doesn't change according to our ability to stomach it.[4] Claiming that we don't want to push our values on others is akin to saying we don't want to push our value of *don't rob banks* on those robbers who might really need some extra cash right about now.

It's enough to make you scream or cry or tear your hair out—that abortion, which is so clearly allowing anti-women policies and customs to flourish, is waved as a rallying flag for feminists today.

And yet . . .

When people have beef with the wider pro-life community, *I get it.*

No one gets more frustrated with pro-life people than other pro-life people. The divisions within one phrase—*pro-life*—are as vast and wide as any political divides. However, there are several issues within the pro-life community that tend to yank it further from Christ and more toward yelling.

One is an overall lack of love, charity, and empathy. Yes, we believe that abortion takes innocent life. But as Paul says in 1 Corinthians 13:1, "If I speak in human and angelic tongues but do not have love, I am a resounding gong or a clashing cymbal." We can all think of a few pro-life friends or family members who are gongs and cymbals, can't we? Kindness is so underrated in today's society. *Love, respect,* and *charity* are seen as things that are nice bonuses but a little old-fashioned and not useful. But they're the most useful tools we have. We forget that Jesus told us again and again to love people, to treat them well, to not be the first to cast stones. I would never discourage someone from sharing the truth of what abortion is and what it does to women. But I'll discourage you faster than you can say "Babies have heartbeats at six weeks!" if you start waving around photos of mangled fetuses outside abortion clinics. Hear?

I'm always aghast when I see internet conversations (oh, internet) dealing with abortion. There's usually more than a handful of comments from Catholics tsk-tsking women and reminding them to keep their legs closed. Some of us have clear-ly forgotten that (a) it takes two to, um, tango, and (b) facing an unplanned pregnancy is one of the hardest, scariest, most intimidating things a woman can go through. So throwing the past back in their faces doesn't exactly scream *love of Christ*. I understand that pro-life Catholics feel—and probably rightly so—that they've lost some sort of culture war and now have to stand stronger and firmer than ever before. But as someone who has stood strong and firm, who has written for very liberal publications and spoken on very liberal podcasts about believing abortion is never, ever okay, I say that you can do so in a loving, charitable way. It's not up to you to turn the tide of the culture. It's up to you to do right by your neighbors and your family.

Another issue is that pro-life groups often forget to provide any lifelong resources. A hug and a word of encouragement are only going to take a woman facing an unplanned pregnancy so far. If we're really interested in lowering the abortion rate, we need to start looking at the root of why women choose abortion: a belief that motherhood simply isn't an option.

Within the Church, mothers are often (rightly so) beloved. We look to Mary as the Queen of Heaven, our parishes offer laundry lists of activities for moms, and fertility is constantly affirmed as a beautiful gift. I'd never felt such an intense sense of community as I did when I became a mother; there were playgroups and prayer meetings and email lists. Being a *mom* was a prize worthy of heaven, something that led to friendships, sainthood, and blessings aplenty. When I had a baby, women I barely knew brought me freezer meals and diapers, and they invited me to Bible studies. People within the Church see motherhood as vital.

That's not always so in society.

Out in the secular world, I know women who have been forced to pump breastmilk for newborns in bathrooms because their offices (illegally) didn't want to provide them rooms. Businesses eschew paid maternity leave because it's a "waste of money" to pay women who aren't actively working, often not

thinking through the logical consequences of such actions—
that women, with their many talents and gifts, won't be able to
succeed within those organizations. Childcare costs continue
to skyrocket, making the idea of being a working mother seem
even more unfeasible. Health care remains incredibly expensive,
and carrying and mothering children requires frequent visits to
doctors, ultrasound techs, and pediatricians. The Church loves
mothers even harder because the secular world so often doesn't.

One organization that focuses on providing lifelong resources to mothers is the Elizabeth House, a nonprofit program of
Care Net Pregnancy Center in my hometown of Madison, Wisconsin. This program houses single mothers for a year, during
which they provide everything from finance education to nutrition lessons to baby clothes. This and other similar programs
allow women to set up sustainable lives for themselves, instead
of just waving a "Development of a Fetus" pamphlet in their faces
and calling it a day. They say "you can" instead of "you should."
We desperately need more programs like this that walk with
women through this difficult journey instead of judging them
for seeking a way out. It's hard for me to believe your pro-life
desires are genuine if you stop caring about a mother and baby
the minute the baby is actually born.

Feminists for Life, a nonpartisan organization that views
abortion as a symptom of a problem rather than the solution
for one, sums it up nicely: "As pro-life employers and educators, we must examine our own policies and practices in our
own communities, workplaces, colleges, and universities. With
woman-centered problem solving, we can set the example for the
nation and the world. We must ramp up efforts to systemically
address the unmet needs of struggling parents, birthparents, and
victims of domestic violence and sexual assault."[5]

Another point of division: adoption. There are numerous
issues with both the system and the way it's spoken about.

I have a friend who has struggled with infertility throughout her marriage. It's a heartbreakingly awful thing to have to go through. One of the most frustrating things she's encountered is people telling her to *just adopt*, as if you can whip into the Adoption Center conveniently located next to your neighborhood Starbucks and pick up a baby of your choice. I imagine birth mothers can feel a similar way, with *just choose adoption* seeming like a picture-perfect and easy answer for us staunch pro-lifers and an achingly difficult choice for those who are actually pregnant. Going through nine months of heartburn and nausea, all leading up to a potential heartbreak and a scar that may never fully heal? There's nothing "just" about it.

If you want to help lower the rate of abortions, a "Defund Planned Parenthood" filter over your profile picture will do much less than donating to a fundraiser for an adoption, volunteering at an informational adoption seminar, or praying alongside women in the muddy waters of this difficult choice. Adoption is incredibly complicated and difficult. But it doesn't end a life. It begins a new family.

One of the most inspiring saints within the Catholic Church that feminists proudly laud as our own is St. Gianna Molla. An Italian physician—how's that for feminist?—Gianna was also a mama to three littles. When she was pregnant with her fourth, her doctors found a fibroma in her uterus, meaning she had a tumor alongside her sweet babe. After being encouraged to pursue an abortion, St. Gianna refused.

She died. Her child lived.

Secular feminists may point to this and say, "See? See how a lack of abortion hurts women?"

Catholic feminists point to this and say, "See? See how we have an infinite capability within us to choose the good of another, to live out the most sacrificial form of love and meet Jesus in heaven after making the most difficult choice a person can make?"

Abortion says, "You can't do this. This is too hard. You don't have the resources, you don't have the partner, you don't have the strength."

The Church whispers, "You can. You do. You are."

But being pro-life means a lot more than being anti-abortion.

Truly pro-life people care for life in all its forms, in all its circumstances, in all its difficulties. Pro-life people care about the lives of the unborn, the elderly, and the homeless. Pro-life people care for the veterans, the sick, and the atheists. Pro-life people care for people, period.

To truly be pro-life you must move beyond that pro-birth mentality. You have to identify who in society is being failed and neglected and commit to caring for them yourself. Pope Francis writes,

> Our defense of the innocent unborn, for example, needs to be clear, firm and passionate, for at stake is the dignity of a human life, which is always sacred and demands love for each person, regardless of his or her stage of development. Equally sacred, however, are the lives of the poor, those already born, the destitute, the abandoned and the underprivileged, the vulnerable infirm and elderly exposed to covert euthanasia, the victims of human trafficking, new forms of slavery, and every form of rejection. We cannot uphold an ideal of holiness that would ignore injustice in a world where some revel, spend with abandon and live only for the latest consumer goods, even as others look on from afar, living their entire lives in abject poverty.[6]

Catholic feminists in particular have to be alert when it comes to the different ways in which members of society can be marginalized. As Catholics we're called to see in each person the likeness of God. That means that the problems of a sex-trafficking victim halfway across the world or the homeless woman down the street? Those are my problems too. From the woman on death row to the woman on CSPAN, these women are *all* part of my tribe; they're daughters of God, whether they know it or not. I have a duty to care for them, to fight for their well-being, and to not turn a blind eye to their lack of resources. What we do for the least of these is what we do for Jesus (Mt 25:40).

The Catholic Church is one of the most charitable organizations in the world. Catholic Charities USA was the eleventh largest source of charitable giving in 2017, according to *Forbes*.[7] According to the *Catholic Herald UK*,

> The Church operates more than 140,000 schools, 10,000 orphanages, 5,000 hospitals and some 16,000 other health clinics. Caritas, the umbrella organization for Catholic aid agencies, estimates that spending by its affiliates totals between £2 billion and £4 billion, making it one of the biggest aid agencies in the world. Even these numbers only tell half the tale. Caritas does not include development spending by a host of religious orders and other Catholic charities, while most of the 200,000 Catholic parishes around the world operate their own small-scale charitable projects which are never picked up in official figures. Establishing like-for-like comparisons is hard, but there can be little doubt that in pretty much every field of social action, from education to health to social care, the Church is the largest and most significant non-state organization in the world.[8]

So the Church is showing up. It *has* been showing up.

One pro-life topic that causes quite the political divide within the Church is that of immigration. When politicians call for borders, the Church has consistently called for bridges. In 2018, the eight bishops whose dioceses make up the southern border of the United States cosigned a statement affirming the dignity and humanity of immigrants and asking the government to understand their plight. I question how truly pro-life people would simply shrug their shoulders and point to an economy that might not be able to support an influx of immigrants as they acquiesce to such borders. It confuses me how truly pro-life people would not mind families being torn apart as deportations rise. I seek to listen and understand, but within that seeking I want to hear more care for families and less care for job statistics. I want to hear people express an understanding that the life of the immigrant is just as worthy, important, and necessary as their own.

Another topic that raises fists and fights within the pro-life community is the death penalty. Here, too, the Church has long had wisdom. Pope Francis recently announced that the death penalty is *never* acceptable—it's a big fat no-no.[9] This is an important reminder of why it's important to worship Christ instead of politicians—some of the most "pro-life" politicians are staunch advocates of the death penalty. But if that's your brand of pro-life, you're truly more anti-abortion. If you see a prisoner as worth less than a fetus, you're deviating from our call to love the most broken among us. How could pro-life people want to rob Paul of the chance of being blinded in Damascus? How could pro-life people hand the government the power to kill when they insist that's what all their pro-choice political opponents are doing?

Another important aspect of our pro-life mentality should be to think of women whose lives look radically different than ours, whether that be by nature of their skin color, abilities, or poverty level. Women of color, for example, encounter very real dilemmas every day that white women will never understand unless we ask. My pro-life mentality, just like my feminism, can't leave anyone behind. It brings along the problems of black women, Latina women, Asian women, and every shade in between. It views the racism that affects my sisters as something that affects me.

Catholic feminism, my feminism, is one that has room for stay-at-home moms who turn on *Daniel Tiger's Neighborhood* for fifteen minutes of peace, nuns who wear habits instead of halter tops, and nurses who know everything from how much epinephrine someone needs to which hospital refrigerator has the best flavored popsicles. Catholic feminism loves female engineers, female janitors, female foster parents, female senators. Catholic feminism loves, period.

Pro-life should be more than a rallying cry; it should be more than a slogan on a bumper sticker or tank top. It should be more than abortion, capital punishment, and immigration. It isn't a set of laws but a state of mind and heart—one that consistently puts people over profit and puts those people on equal footing. To be pro-life means to avoid wishing harm on others and to instead put them first.

The world doesn't need more anger, more selfishness, more what's-mine-is-mine mentality. The world needs powerful, strong, empathetic love. And that, my sister, is what we can bring to the table.

Six

Loving Jesus

Listen, sister: The Church is my family. And just like my actual family, I love it fiercely and dearly. I'll protect it from anything the world tries to throw at it. My loyalty knows no bounds.

And just like my actual family, sometimes I want to punch it in the face.

My husband has commented multiple times on the fact that he doesn't understand my relationship with my sister. She's my best friend. I talk with her almost daily, texting her anything from the minute details about my latest purchase to my toddler's occasionally abhorrent behavior. We send each other animojis of song lyrics. We drive across the country on spontaneous road trips (well, we did before I had children). We sing Dixie Chicks songs at the top of our lungs, to the annoyance of anyone within a fifty-foot radius. She was my maid of honor and is our number one babysitter. There's truly nobody with whom I would rather hang out.

And oh, that girl can piss me off like no other. Nobody can get under my skin with a rude comment or well-placed eye roll quite like my sister. We fight hard and passionately, tossing around angry words we'd never dare say to a friend. I'll be practically snarling at her like a rabid animal, and then ten minutes later we'll be calmly debating the best season of *Gilmore Girls*. She is my

Person—the person who knows me better than anyone, who is quick to forgive my many flaws, and who loves me unconditionally through anything. When someone's there for almost every up and down of your life, the type of relationship that develops includes a deep, unbreakable love and understanding.

This is similar in many ways to my relationship with the Church. The Church is my home and lifeblood. Nothing keeps me calmer and nothing gets me more worked up. When you love something that much, it has the potential to get you the angriest. You want it to thrive, not to starve itself with petty arguments. You want it to do what you know it's meant to do.

You'd think the formal structure of the Catholic Church would eliminate any divisions. Like, we have a pope, y'all! He'll tell us what to do and how to act. Just listen to your priest. Follow the Bible. One, two, tie my shoe—we'll get this all figured out and it will all be so simple.

Ha.

Anyone who's been Catholic or around Catholic people for longer than five seconds knows that this is a pipe dream. If you get four Catholics in a room, you'll have four opinions on everything ranging from proper hymns for Mass to voting priorities to whether or not you can eat meat on Fridays. You have hip, young millennial Catholics, baby boomers who lived through Vatican II, social justice–focused Catholics, pro-life Catholics, Catholic feminists, #trads (not sure what this means, but I sure see it on Twitter a lot), Catholics who love FOCUS, Catholics who love Jesuits, and Catholics who will only go to Latin Mass. There are Catholics who veil, Catholics who wear jeans to Mass, single Catholics, and Catholics with twelve kids. We're one Church, but we've got a whole lot of members, and those members clash and collaborate in a myriad of ways.

But we have a great gift that keeps our diverse members together: the *Catechism of the Catholic Church*. It's a handy-dandy book that lovingly reminds us of Catholic teachings and rules that must be followed. We have guidelines, and they're part of what makes us different from other Christians. These rules may seem suffocating, until you realize what a blessed gift it is to be instructed by the Church and not have to make every little decision by your own wayward heart. It's so popular in our culture to toss the phrase "listen to your heart" around, but I disagree. My heart has a temper. It seeks revenge and arguments. It often wants to be snarky and sarcastic. The thing can't be trusted all the time. That's why we have intellect, a brain that can comprehend complex teachings and implement them in our own lives. The guidelines the *Catechism* sets forth bring me so much peace.

Within those guidelines, however, are a thousand shades of gray. Like the *Catechism* says, you have to attend Mass on Sundays.

Okay, that's pretty clear.

But do you have to take Communion on the tongue, or is it okay to take it in your hands? How sick do you have to be before you can miss Mass? How obnoxiously loud do your children have to scream before you deposit them in the nursery? Are yoga pants acceptable Mass attire? If you aren't really paying attention during the Gospel but instead are mentally creating a grocery list, did you really go to Mass? Can you accept the Eucharist from a layperson? Is it better to sit near the front or the back, near the middle or the aisle? How bad of a state of sin does your soul have to be in before you don't get the Eucharist? If you don't get the Eucharist, is that okay? On and on and on and on, an endless series of debates, everyone trying to one-up and out-Catholic the other; everyone claiming that the harder thing is the holier thing; everyone forgetting that one of the most beautiful gifts our Church gives us is room to wiggle within steadfast rules so that we can live out our faith in a way that most aligns with our conscience, abilities, and temperament.

But remembering those things is so much less fun than proving how holy we are, right? Judging others is our second language. We tell ourselves we're holding others to a high bar, that we're delivering them the truth, but in all actuality we're acting like Pharisees to our little hearts' content. It feels *good* to put others in their place, the way eating twelve cookies feels good. For a moment it gives us a *thump* of satisfaction, but in a few minutes we realize what we just did was incredibly stupid. But when we judge others, we aren't just being stupid; we're being cruel.

There are times I feel so ridiculously frustrated with our Church. Sometimes it's when people throw shade at Pope Francis, accusing him of not being as theologically articulate as Pope Benedict XVI or leading people astray. Sometimes it's when I meet Catholics who off-handedly mention that they don't go to Mass because their priest is too boring or not focused enough on the issue of their choice. But the times I feel most annoyed, when I truly start to pray that we haven't completely lost our way, are when I'm surfing through Catholic Land in social media. I recently had to take a Twitter hiatus because I realized that when I read the Act of Contrition during Confession, I'm promising to avoid things that lead me to sin, and a place where everyone tries to be the wittiest and smartest in 140 characters is definitely a pathway to hell for a prideful millennial such as myself.

When I'm in those moments with my brothers and sisters in Christ, when I feel like a lost little sheep with no shepherd but a whole lot of self-righteous anger, I return to Jesus.

I take my Bible, a faded leather thing stuffed with notes from former students and current friends. I open it to the gospels because they speak the gentlest to me. I was a journalism major in college so I appreciate reliable reporting, and when Luke opens up his gospel with a promise that everything has been clearly investigated so that the reader can trust the truth of what he says, my heart pitter-patters.

And then I read what Jesus has to say:

"Stop judging, that you may not be judged. For as you judge, so will you be judged, and the measure with which you measure will be measured out to you" (Mt 7:1–2).

"For the Son of Man did not come to destroy men's lives, but to save them" (Lk 9:56, NASB).

"Take care to guard against all greed; for though one may be rich, one's life does not consist of possessions" (Lk 12:15).

The parable of the good Samaritan, the parable of the prodigal son—in these I find Jesus over and over again. I don't find him often on Instagram, in the *Huffington Post*, or on podcasts, although I'm sure he's there. I find him in Mass. I find him in frozen lasagnas brought after babies are born, in emails from old students who have started young adult movements in their parishes, in the sight of a wiggly toddler stretched into a lion costume for Halloween. But mostly I find him in scripture.

When I hear Catholics say things about women's intellectual inferiority, about how women really need to learn to cover up our shoulders, or about how women are just too dang sensitive to embark on any real leadership, I read what Jesus had to say about women. I look at how he interacted with them. I look at his friendships, kindness, and compassion, and I'm *reminded* of the truth: Jesus thought women had more to offer the world than a skirt and a smile; Jesus believed women could be dreamers, students, and evangelists. It's a truth that doesn't change, no matter how many YouTube commenters think it should. Terrible things happen to women all over the world every single day—they're bought and sold; abused, raped, and neglected—but Jesus, *he is still good.*

I could weep, sitting in this coffee shop as I write, over how much I love that man.

I have a friend who used to just sigh and say "Jesus is real" constantly. Someone quit Bible study? "Jesus is real." Someone made a comment about her butt in a bar? "Jesus is real." Someone she thought she trusted betrayed her? "Jesus is real." It sounds flippant, but it was anything but. It was a constant reminder of the reality of our world: we've already *been* saved, and one day we'll spend eternity in heaven with Jesus. All of that other crap just really, truly doesn't matter because Jesus is real. So if you think I'm a bleeding heart or an anti-women redneck, I honestly don't care, because Jesus is real. And if I know Jesus, nothing can touch me.

If you're feeling as if the Church has transformed into your enemy, it hasn't. I promise. But maybe you need to take a step back and reconnect with Jesus. Maybe your community needs to shrink a bit to just you and Jesus, sitting in the early morning light with a cup of coffee, a pen, and a prayer. When I'm confronted by people arguing over what Jesus would want us to do, instead of jumping into the argument I simply ask Jesus. He usually makes it pretty clear.

One of the blessings of our Church is the accessibility of the community it offers. If your thing is mom's group, or parish council, or the intermural volleyball league—awesome. Those things will be waiting for you when you get right with Jesus. Your favorite Catholic blog or Catholic Twitter user probably isn't going away. Once you recenter yourself in that relationship with Christ, you can dive back into community feeling more deeply rooted and harder to shake. I think it would do us all a world of good to disappear for a moment now and then, to realize we don't have to constantly volunteer, attend, and engage. Sometimes we need to recharge our batteries with the gospels and a highlighter. Then we can pour into others that much better and stand firm against naysayers or unnecessary drama.

Sisters, we can't have Catholic feminism without Jesus. We simply can't. As he says, "I am the true vine, and my Father is the vine grower. He takes away every branch in me that does not bear fruit, and every one that does he prunes so that it bears more fruit. You are already pruned because of the word that I spoke to you. Remain in me, as I remain in you. Just as a branch cannot bear fruit on its own unless it remains on the vine, so neither can you unless you remain in me" (Jn 15:1–4). We can't produce good fruit apart from him. Even Pope Francis, a fierce advocate for social justice, warned Catholics against forgetting to put Christ at the center of our actions lest the Church "end up a compassionate NGO."[1] In the same homily, he compared building on things other than a love for Christ, "like when children make sandcastles and then it all falls down."[2] Our Catholic faith, our relationship with Jesus, has to be front and center of our feminism and our social justice efforts. If we aren't seeing people as made in the image of Christ, we aren't seeing them properly. Our efforts will result in feel-good feelings or superficial fixes. It will stop being about truly loving humanity. We were made for God, by God, which means we were made for love, by love. We can't ever forget that.

Take today's sexuality culture combined with some Christians' purity culture. One part of the world tells us that sex is the greatest thing we can have and that the most empowering thing we can do is to have as many sexual partners as possible. On the other hand, many Christian women are brought up being taught that the worst thing they can possibly do is have sex before marriage, and that if they do, they're damaged goods. Which is Catholic? Which is feminist? Isn't there a stance that allows us to respect what sex is truly for while still not valuing our bodies' purity above all else?

Instead of getting caught up in the tangled web of hurt, turn to what Jesus says:

That you aren't goods but a daughter of Abraham (see Luke 13:16).

That you're worthy of learning and being a disciple (see Luke 10:42).

That the ones without sin should cast the first stone (see John 8:7).

Jesus reminds us of the truth again and again and again. So how can we tangibly stay connected with God and his Son? Through one of the Church's greatest gifts: the sacraments.

Within the Catholic Church and within her sacraments we have something incredible. We have the true presence of Jesus in tangible ways. We aren't simply calling up prayers to a pie-in-the-sky Lord; we're interacting with him, touching him, *seeing him*.

This is insane.

Obviously something that sets Catholics apart is our Eucharist. We don't view Communion as something to be celebrated once a month, with whatever bread we pick up at the grocery store and some grape juice. Our Eucharist is sacred. It's rooted in Jesus' words recorded in Scripture: "I am the bread of life. Your ancestors ate the manna in the desert, but they died; this is the bread that comes down from heaven so that one may eat it and not die. I am the living bread that came down from heaven; whoever eats this bread will live forever; and the bread that I will give is my flesh for the life of the world" (Jn 6:48–51, NABRE).

Some of the followers of Jesus freak out. They think, *This Jesus has taken things too far. We're down with loving our neighbors, with caring for the poor, but eating the flesh of Jesus? This is freaky.* And people leave, prompting Jesus to ask his disciples if they plan on bailing too.

But the true disciples stick around. They see the Eucharist for what it is: a gift. And during the Last Supper, when Jesus institutes the Eucharist he bestows upon us a way to remain close to him through famines, Twitter wars, and poorly spent Church funds. He gives us a way to abide in him. We Catholics *love* the Eucharist, the "source and summit" of our faith (*CCC*, 1324). It's both where we come from and what we strive for. We can partake of it every day.

The United States Council of Catholic Bishops says that "while our sins would have made it impossible for us to share in the life of God, Jesus Christ was sent to remove this obstacle. His death was a sacrifice for our sins. Christ is 'the Lamb of God, who takes away the sin of the world' (Jn 1:29). Through his death and resurrection, he conquered sin and death and reconciled us to God. The Eucharist is the memorial of this sacrifice."[3] This means that even though we're so ridiculously unworthy, God extends his hands out to us and welcomes us back again and again.

Without the Sacrament of the Eucharist, our faith will falter. It's tempting to say that Jesus doesn't want us sitting in church when we could be out loving our families or caring for the poor. But take it from Mother Teresa, whom no one can argue didn't do her fair share of caring for the poor: she spent at least an hour in front of Jesus in the Eucharist daily and required that her fellow Missionaries of Charity do the same. She understood that she couldn't pour into others if she didn't first allow Christ to pour into her.

Another sacrament that consistently keeps Jesus at the forefront of our minds is that of Confession. If we're living in states of mortal sin, how can we possibly serve our fellow brothers and sisters? Plucking the wood out of our own eye before correcting the problems of the world is essential. I once asked a priest if hearing confessions for hours upon end during a Lenten penance service made him sad—after all, it's sin upon sin upon sin, hours and hours of humanity's worst moments. He looked me in the eyes and said, dead seriously, "Hearing hours of confessions is the happiest thing I get to do as a priest. It's like kicking Satan in the face every time." To allow our Lord to wash our sins away, to take part in the greatness of salvation history? This is a precious responsibility we've been given. I remember one particularly rough confession in college where I had *quite* the list of sins, so many that I had to literally write them out and bring in a piece of paper. I was certain the priest was going to open up a can of verbal whoop-ass on me. Instead, he said with every ounce of joy, "Praise God. You keep making confessions like that and you'll become a saint."

I'll take it.

Confession, Fr. Mike Schmitz says, is where the "desire to impress goes to die."[4] It's us at our most humble. When I feel too on-top-of-the-world, like some sort of badass world changer, Confession is where I remember that I'm dust. Confession reminds me of my pride and anger, my weaknesses and demons. Confession reminds me that I'm a pretty imperfect wife and mom, that I don't love nearly enough, that I'm actually pretty selfish. Confession knocks me off my high horse and down to the arms of Jesus. There's something so sweetly freeing about naming your sins aloud and knowing that you've been forgiven. It's the very essence of our faith: that we can be made new.

Here is what our Church gives *you*, sweet sister, so frustrated you can barely speak. The Church gives you prayers.

I'm well aware that this is actually something that makes many run from the Church. Our given prayers feel so formulaic and stiff. They're not as fun or fancy as freestyling it with a rock-and-roll band behind you. They feel formal and enclosed, as if we're following a script. But there have been times in my life where these ritualistic prayers have saved me.

The Rosary, the Our Father, the Divine Mercy Chaplet—these whispered scripts can be so beautiful. There's something to be said for saying words that have been said millions of times before you. We've all gotten to the point of frustration with God where we can barely speak. It's times like those when prewritten prayers come most in handy. The Rosary in particular is something with which I had to get over an annoyance. It's long and dry, and honestly, I didn't "get anything" out of it. (I'm not quite sure what this phrase even means—was I waiting for a white dove of the Holy Spirit to burst out of the sky and land on my shoulder? An overwhelming sense of joy that made my skin tingle? A vision of Mary four feet from my eyes? No clue.) But the simple repetition of talking to our mama has brought me so much peace in times when I didn't know what else to say. When you see chemical weapons being used on TV or priests from the Church you love going to jail for abuse, it's sometimes all you can do to say, "Mom? Help."

I used to think that the repetitive nature of the Rosary made it less effective; that since we're all just mumbling along, we don't really mean the words. But then I had kids. And I tell those wiggly, wild-thing kids that I love them eighty million times a day. I say it because they just woke up or they picked up their toys or I caught their eye in the rearview mirror or they handed me a stuffed animal or they just looked particularly cute at the moment. It just bursts out of me, randomly and often. And I mean it every single time.

So these things that make us different from our Protestant sisters—the Eucharist, Confession, and our prayers—these things that so many see as ritualistic, unnecessary, or dull? They're what give power to our mission. I've met many women who claim they're better able to find God in nature than in a church building. While I certainly believe God can whisper among the pine trees, I don't believe the Eucharist spontaneously bursts out of the ocean. I believe the hard, noble work of showing up on Sunday—whether it's to a beautiful basilica, a Newman Center chapel, or a 1970s wood-paneled neighborhood church— is essential. I believe saying the prayers we've been taught for years and years will strengthen us. And I believe kneeling down in a carpeted confessional will cleanse us.

Attending church isn't as pithy, fun, or Instagram-worthy as a place you can bring a latte. It doesn't give us all the feels that wiping down a table at a soup kitchen does. But it's important because church, that place that at times can feel stale and seden- tary, is where we go to connect with the source of all life. It's *real*. There's surely someone who will look you in the eyes and tell you that, as a Catholic, you're far from Jesus, but that's a lie. You know Jesus. You know him well. As Paul writes, "For I am convinced that neither death, nor life, nor angels, nor principalities, nor present things, nor future things, nor powers, nor height, nor depth, nor any other creature will be able to separate us from the love of God in Christ Jesus our Lord" (Rom 8:38–39).

It can be so frustrating to belong to a Church made of broken humans, can't it? I mean, really. Fix it, Jesus. I got to a point during one particular election cycle—yup, you know the one—where I had just about had it. I didn't want to be part of the Church I was seeing, the one that yelled and snarked and looked so little like Jesus to me. If I saw one more YouTube video of an angry priest telling us who to vote for, I was going to scream. If I had to have one more conversation about whether or not we should hold hands during the Our Father while politicians argued about what was worse, ending the lives of children through abortion or ending the lives of children by slamming our borders closed, I was going to throw a Bible at someone.

But this Church, as angry as its members can make me, is the only one with the fullness of truth. I know that the way I know the sun will rise, even if its teachings can confuse me and its members can cause me to cuss.

Because somewhere squished between cynicism and self-doubt, political ramblings and trolls, hashtags and declarations, there's truth. Jesus and the Church he founded are my home. And I, like Peter, don't know to whom else I could go.

And when you find yourself worrying about things such as which way the priest should face during the consecration or whether or not people are allowed to hold hands during the Our Father; things such as who the priest thinks you should vote for or if money should go to orphan care, CCD class, or finally fixing that parking lot pothole, you grab your bible and go back to Jesus.

He is our Person.

seven

Loving Your Vocation

I still remember the day I found out that the Catholic Church teaches that artificial contraception is immoral.

Did I learn this in CCD classes, from my university's Catholic center, or from my own family? No. I learned it at a huge conference for Catholic college students, where eight thousand of us waited in line at crappy hotel coffee shops, and sat in folding chairs for Mass and talks about evangelization. One of the speakers referenced the Church's teaching on birth control, and as I looked around I realized something daunting.

She was *serious*, and many people agreed with her.

I grew up casually Catholic. I didn't realize nuns still wore habits. I thought Confession was a cute thing you did in fourth grade and then probably never again. Didn't Jesus say something about the crazy people always being among us or wolves in sheep's clothing or something? Surely he meant people who thought condom manufacturers were in league with the devil.

I should also probably add that I'd been on birth control for, like, seven years at this point.

I knew I wanted kids, but I also knew I didn't want seven of them, back-to-back-to-back. To me, it seemed as if the only way to prevent that was hormonal birth control. Surely—*surely*—our sweet Church wouldn't hold these magical pills just out of reach.

As we walked out of the talk, I turned to one of my friends and said in a hushed tone, "Wait, people actually think that?"

She turned to me and I saw it in her eyes: *Oh, girl, we've got some work to do together.*

There are plenty of things to make fun of Catholics for, from our funny chant-like prayers to that whole "Eucharist as cannibalism" misunderstanding. But the Church's teaching on contraception remains one of its hardest to swallow. The jokes about the Catholic families with ten kids are endless. Women with more than 2.5 smiling kids at Mass are either scorned (because, *hello*, overpopulation) or held up as pinnacles of society (good Catholic women understand that the goal of life is bearing as many children as possible, no matter the cost!). Women with less than 2.5 smiling kids at Mass are either nodded at approvingly for helping with population control or judged silently by those "real" Catholics who know "grave reason"—the only reason to use natural family planning to try to not get pregnant—means *life or death.*

The day we stop silently judging the women around us will be a happy day indeed. Fix it, Jesus.

Like so many Church teachings, the more I studied it, the more it began to make sense. The Church believes that sex is for (a) pleasure and (b) babies, and although sex doesn't always result in babies (just like it doesn't always result in pleasure), we still can't dismiss the act from its possible effect.

In Pope Paul VI's encyclical on the regulation of birth, *Humanae Vitae*, he makes a few fundamental predictions about what will happen to society if we embrace artificial contraception. One is that men will be driven to "reduce her to being a mere instrument for the satisfaction of his own desires, no longer considering her as his partner whom he should surround with care and affection."[1] Another is that public authorities will begin pushing birth control on citizens. (China's one-child policy comes to mind, as do recent US lawsuits about religious freedoms.) A third is that infidelity and sexual immorality will rise. While there's no way to study this, I wager that hookup culture dominates our society, particularly among college-aged men and women. When sex comes so cheaply, with so little responsibility attached to it, of course it's spent more frequently and unnecessarily.

Then there's the science. One of the beautiful things about our Church is that, contrary to popular belief, it works hand in hand with science and God's order. According to a 2016 study, there's a 40 percent increased risk of depression after six months of birth control pill usage.[2] A 2017 study found that women who use hormonal birth control were three times more likely to attempt suicide than women who don't use hormonal birth control.[3] A 2018 study found that women who used hormonal contraceptives had a 20 percent increased risk of breast cancer.[4]

I hear story after story of women who went off the pill after it made them feel "crazy" or "overly hormonal." Not that we should base medicine off anecdotal evidence, but if you find ten women on birth control pills and ask them about how it affects their mood, I wager you'll find a similar response.

When I was on birth control I spent seven years with shining skin and no cramps. Our friendly modern medical system tends to hand out birth control pills to teenage girls like lollipops. I'm not saying the pill has zero positive side effects but rather that it's frequently used as a bandage for major medical issues, has a negative effect on the mental health of women, and allows sex to be enjoyed with less intention. As a feminist I can't support things that lead women to despair just to make life superficially easier.

So what does any of this have to do with vocation?

A *vocation*, meaning a *call*, is typically used within the Church as how God is calling you to live out your family life. Vocations include religious life, married life, and single life. If you're called to the vocation of marriage, you're in the majority. That's where I hang out.

Let me be clear: every single vocation has its struggles. Religious sisters are called to radical lifestyles; depending on their order, they're bound to strict schedules, instructed to give up all their possessions, and live lives of chastity. Single women can often be plagued with feelings of loneliness and are probably the most overlooked vocationally—many people don't understand that singleness can bring women to heaven just as much as any other vocation. Married women have to live in community with men who probably drive them nuts quite a bit (love you, Krzysztof) and have to figure out how to balance a sex life with appropriate family planning. No vocation is given a get-out-of-suffering-free card, no matter how much time you spend dreaming of escaping to a tropical island by yourself or perusing precious family Christmas cards on Pinterest.

Family planning was a struggle in my vocation that I had to wrap my head around. The Church permits natural family planning as a way to plan your family while inviting God into the picture. There are many methods, but they all involve some type of fertility tracking and abstinence on fertile days. This comes with its own set of struggles. For starters, many women don't have textbook menstruation cycles, and then there's the human factor of having to use major willpower and abstain a few days a month. And while natural family planning is constantly being hailed as "beautiful," "marriage building," and "scientifically proven" (all true!), it can all become very eye-roll inducing when you're trying to decipher cervical mucus and wondering if your uterus can really handle an inhabitant. Although I could go on for days about the importance of women understanding their bodies and respecting their fertility instead of acting as if their bodies and fertility are something shameful that must be avoided at all costs, I can't lie and say I've never wondered just how bad contraception really is. I mean, it's popping a pill, not robbing a bank.

But we don't embrace Church teachings because they're easy to swallow, socially acceptable, or make us feel good. We embrace them because they're true. As Jenny Uebbing writes on the blog *Mama Needs Coffee*:

> Here's the thing though; Jesus doesn't promise convenience, lack of suffering, or predictability. There was something about a cross and lifting it upright and you know the rest.
>
> We live in a time and a place where convenience is the highest good. I think some of us actually worship it. I think of this most often when I'm doing the microwave dance, reheating my morning coffee, wondering how twenty-eight seconds can pass so slowly and, if I stare intently at this glowing box, will it heat any faster? But Christianity is not convenient.[5]

Sex, even within marriage, isn't simply for our own pleasure. It's for mirroring the love of God and participating in his plans for the world, to demonstrate fruitfulness, love, and an openness to life.

Being a feminist within your vocation can seem counterintuitive. But vocations are calls to love and serve. All of us are called within our unique vocations to serve others, which, as we discussed previously, is a fundamental tenet of womanhood. So just like we have to get over the idea that service within our community means mopping the floors (although it might!), we also have to get over the idea that service within our vocations, particularly marriage (don't worry, single women, we'll get to you in a minute), means saying "yes, honey" to whatever our husbands suggest. Just as women are called to love and honor their husbands, husbands are called to love and honor their wives as Christ honors the Church (see Ephesians 5:22–27).

It's not always easy to be a strong, moxie-filled woman who still honors and respects her husband. I certainly don't let my husband wield decision-making power like a king wields a crown. But for me, honoring and respecting means listening, caring, and seeking to understand. These things don't come naturally to me. They require stretching and reaching. But if part of the definition of moxie includes *courage*, we must have the courage to admit that we don't have all the answers and aren't always right.

My husband and I are both a bit . . . well, spicy. Stubborn. One of our favorite questions to ask our couple friends is, what is the stupidest fight you've ever had? The answers usually leave all of us in fits of laughter, because who hasn't gotten into knock-down-drag-'em-out fights about forgotten groceries, misplaced library books, and awkwardly hung picture frames? But we once asked another married couple for their stupidest fight and their response was to simply look at each other and shrug. "We don't really fight," they said.

Never have Krzysztof or I laughed so hard in our lives—not at them; at ourselves—because the good Lord knows that is *not* the marriage we're in.

We fight. We always make up. However, we don't have the type of marriage that involves subtle sighs and shrugs of *whatever*. Ours can involve slammed doors and swear words at times. Our problem-solving methods could use some work. But a moxie-marriage isn't one without love, forgiveness, or sacrifice. To us, love doesn't mean swallowing solutions without often rigorous debate beforehand. Krzysztof listens to what I have to say. I do the same to him. We're partners. As he's fond of saying, "The man might be the head of the household but the woman is definitely the neck."

Marriage and *wife* don't look one way. We've accepted this about the word *sister*, haven't we? We have religious sisters who are active in their communities—teaching, speaking, and leading. We have religious sisters who work in hospitals, schools, and homeless shelters. We have religious sisters who lead protests and those who live out lives of quiet consecration and prayer. There are religious sisters who sew, clean, bake wafers for use in the Eucharist, care for expecting mothers, and teach Austrian children how to sing.

Why can we not say the same about wives—that there are wives who homeschool their kids; wives who make home-cooked, organic dinners; and wives who are brain surgeons? Wives who watch EWTN, wives who watch *Parenthood*, and wives who avoid screen time for their families? Wives who are software engineers, wives who are bloggers, wives who are housekeepers, and wives who are just trying to get through the damn day?

But no. We have to get into fights about how *true* wives are also biological mothers who stay home with their kids, because if Mom goes to work and drops her kids off at daycare, they will be psychologically scarred for years. Or how *true* wives and mothers are out there contributing to society (because child-rearing is, of course, pointless and a waste of a brain) and we need to free those poor stay-at-home moms from their lives of quiet desperation.

Why does every single issue in feminism come down to dichotomies, as if there are two sides entrenched in a deep battle, refusing to believe that God didn't make two kinds of people—the good and the bad?

We need to talk about working women for a second, regardless of their familial vocation. To quote the philosopher Edith Stein, "Every profession in which woman's soul comes into its own and which can be formed by woman's soul is an authentic woman's profession."[6] I understand that children benefit from having their mothers at home the first few years of their lives. However, it would also benefit kids to only eat organic vegetables, never see a television screen, and attend daily holy hours. But those may or may not be realistic for modern families, and they also may or may not be the best choices for modern families.

I feel called to be a mother. I also feel called to work as a freelance writer and podcaster. I don't believe God wants me to let my small children run wild with no supervision, therefore they go to daycare two mornings a week with a friendly, wonderful woman and a gaggle of their buddies. They benefit from the social interaction and love the break from me. Our family benefits from my paychecks and I benefit from stretching my writer muscles. I *want* to work. I *enjoy* it. And what I want and enjoy matters too. It doesn't mean I don't sacrifice as a mother, as I believe I can prove through hundreds of nighttime nursing sessions, a body that has birthed two children, and the lack of a yacht in my nonexistent backyard lake. But I'm an important member of my family, and what's good for me matters too. In the eyes of God I'm as beloved as my children. I have no shame in saying that.

If we truly want women to choose life, to be *empowered* in their decisions as mothers, we have to do a better job at supporting both working mothers and stay-at-home mothers. The vocation of marriage can be lived out in a million ways, and each one should be supported and celebrated. Part of feminism is trusting women to make the best decisions for their families, even if those decisions don't look like the ones you would make yourself. There's more than one option under the umbrella of morality. There isn't simply one archetype of a holy Catholic wife.

But even with all of these pressures on the vocations of marriage and motherhood, I still think there's a vocation that gets less recognition and support. And that's the vocation of singlehood.

As a mom, I'm positively poured into by the Church. There are blogs, podcasts, and books dedicated to helping me be a better Catholic mother. Parishes offer prayer circles, playgroups, and Bible studies. The support is constant, flowing, and much appreciated. Sure, some people frustrate me by acting as if my fertility is the only thing that makes me a woman, but at least they're *talking* about me.

Singleness doesn't receive this support.

I have many friends who are single. This isn't surprising, as I'm a woman in her mid-twenties in modern-day America. But what saddens me is the lack of care for these single women. So many conversations about feminism and womanhood center on marriage and fertility; so few center on the things that *truly* make us women: our callings, our hearts, our intuition. Single women are seen as the people who can volunteer for every single parish activity since, except in unusual circumstances, they don't have kids at home—because God forbid they still have lives to attend to—otherwise they seem to be constantly ignored and forgotten.

There are three types of singleness: (1) women who are called to marriage but are currently in a period of singleness, (2) women who feel called to singleness as a vocation itself, meaning they're living out lives of chastity, and (3) women who were formerly married and are now trying to figure out life as a widow or formerly married person.

All groups of single women are underutilized in the Church. Yes, it's important to serve your parish, but it's also important to understand that those feelings of *For the love, leave me alone for one night, I have no more bake-sale goodies to contribute to you people* are incredibly valid.

Just because single women don't have the stereotypical family unit that members of the Church have deemed ideal doesn't mean they don't have the need for spiritual growth. Specific ministries for women focused on areas others than growing as mothers and wives are essential in parish life. Nearly every parish has a mom's group, but what about a women's group—one that doesn't meet at 10:00 a.m. on Tuesdays, when most single women will likely be working? By constantly holding up marriage as the gold standard and treating single women as "other," we're reinforcing the idea that women were created for men, not as autonomous individuals.

Single women need to embrace boundaries—for example, knowing when they need time for relaxation and leisure and being empowered to say no to being on every single committee. One of my dearest friends worked as a youth minister during her single years and shared with me that she felt as if, since she was one of the only unmarried women at her parish, she should always be the last one to leave work. But feeling as if your relationship status should determine your work hours is nonsensical. Through prayer, proper discernment, and spiritual direction, single women should determine a way of service that doesn't involve raising their hands for every single activity just because they might be available.

Catholics also need to stop viewing singleness as a disease we need to cure. Sure, the Church should provide single young adults opportunities to mix and mingle to help foster holy vocations. But we should also embrace single women exactly as they are, not as projects we're trying to fix. They don't necessarily need men—they need a foundation of spirituality, a love for Christ, and the sacraments, just as married women do.

As for our religious sisters, how can they possibly embrace feminism? Women who choose to eschew possessions and wear habits? It's easy to look at certain groups of sisters, particularly consecrated ones who are tucked away from the outside world, and think that what they do is pointless. But it's undeniable that these sisters who spend hours a day in prayer are boldly serving. If you think giving up your entire life to marry Christ and live in community with other women is anything but courageous and determined, I question your understanding of the definition of *moxie*. Sisters who love, sisters who care, sisters who serve—they understand that women and men are of equal dignity and worth. They're as much feminists as anyone else.

All vocations—familial or career—are called to be holy. We're called to love and serve, no matter what our season of life is.

Pope Francis writes, "Are you called to the consecrated life? Be holy by living out your commitment with joy. Are you married? Be holy by loving and caring for your husband or wife, as Christ does for the Church. Do you work for a living? Be holy by laboring with integrity and skill in the service of your brothers and sisters. Are you a parent or grandparent? Be holy by patiently teaching the little ones how to follow Jesus. Are you in a position of authority? Be holy by working for the common good and renouncing personal gain."[7]

If you're struggling to discern your vocation as a feminist, know this, sister: God wants you to do his will. He'll make it as clear as possible. God doesn't desire your stress or anxiety; he wants only your heart. He's not going to hide his will like a buried treasure and simply hope you stumble upon it. If you're in a season of waiting, it's because he feels it's necessary for your heart. If you're in a season of struggle, it's because he feels it's necessary for your salvation. God wills your good. Period.

No one vocation is called to holiness, servitude, or feminism. We *all* have vocations, and we're all called to live out our faith through them.

eight

Loving Your Neighbor

I've spent a lot of my life not being very loving to my neighbors.

I was once asked on a podcast what I was like in high school, and my immediate response was "the *worst*." I was self-conscious, horrendously so, with the kind of low self-esteem that inspires you to be cruel and conniving. I was too quiet about things that mattered and unbearably loud about things that didn't. "Loving" people meant using them or showing off in fancy ways that I was friends with the right people. I shudder thinking about those four years.

Even in college I wasn't that great at loving my neighbor. I tended to think about what people could *do* for me. I want to go back and slap myself in the face for the cruel, unnecessarily hurtful things I said about the poor, the struggling, and the suffering. But I didn't know Jesus. I thought love meant a Valentine's Day card. I didn't yet realize it really meant Jesus' Cross.

When I first married my husband and moved into his apartment, I was so embarrassed that he could hear me pee. It was the weirdest thing to think about, but I did. Whenever I went to the bathroom, I would squeeze my eyes shut and pretend that maybe, just maybe, he had suddenly become deaf and could go on thinking I was a beautiful unicorn who never had to pee.

Fast-forward a year. I was pregnant with our son, and pregnancy for me was anything but an Instagram-worthy walk in the park. With both of my pregnancies I battled nasty cases of hyperemesis gravidarum, which is similar to feeling incredibly hungover on a good day and throwing up fifteen to twenty times on a bad one. I was hospitalized five times while pregnant as a result of dehydration. It's not fun. And if you've never had the delight of vomiting so hard you pee your pants, you're a luckier woman than I. So there I was, on the floor of our teensy apartment bathroom, simultaneously barfing into a toilet and literally peeing myself on the floor.

Motherhood. It's a beaut.

All embarrassment? Gone. All shame? Out the door. I just looked at my husband and started laughing, and we were both cracking up, so hysterically we could barely catch our breaths. That man has cleaned puke out of carpets, cars, and kitchen tile, and let's just say I'm no longer embarrassed that he might hear me pee.

With my second pregnancy not only did I have horrendous nausea but I also had a toddler who wasn't content to just sit around the house all day. One morning I decided we would try to venture to the store. We were about halfway there when I just lost it—I got sick *everywhere*, on a busy road where I couldn't slam on the brakes or even pull over easily. My poor guy was wailing in the back seat, confused and scared, while I shrieked "It's OK, it's OK, it's OK, Mama is OK!" I pulled off onto a side street and realized we were right by the home of one of my friends, a woman I knew from church. I pulled into her driveway, whipped out my phone, and called her.

"Hey! Are you home? Oh, good. I just projectile vomited in my car and I'm in your driveway and I really, really need you to come outside and grab Benjamin."

Love is having a friend who will help you wipe puke out of your upholstered car seats. You can't overstate the importance of neighbors at a time like that.

That's love. Not a greeting card or a boom box held over your head. I love me a good romantic comedy but I have to admit that half the time I'm watching them I'm thinking, *But would Tom Hanks clean Meg Ryan's pee off a bathroom floor?*

Loving our neighbors doesn't look like simply adding a filter to our Facebook profile picture. It's good, hard, messy work. Having hard conversations, sharing whispered prayers, digging into the places that hurt—those make cleaning vomit out of a car look *easy*. And that's what loving a neighbor looks like.

I'm still not so great at loving my neighbor.

Not my actual neighbors, whose names I can never remember, nor my neighbors on the other side of the world, whom I forget to consider when buying products without checking whether they were ethically made simply because someone is having a sale. Loving my neighbor feels like a nice platitude; it's a reminder not to swear when someone cuts me off in traffic, as if loving my neighbor were a box I could check every day instead of a way to live my life.

But I've seen real, true neighborly love in action. Taking care of our own—this is where the Church in many ways excels. When someone has a baby, she is given casserole after casserole. When someone is sick, candles are lit and prayer cards are filled out. When someone needs prayers, love, or encouragement, the Church meets them where they're at. When someone is broken, a community of faith is there to put them back together. Catholics can do pretty great when it comes to loving other Catholics.

The issue usually comes when the person who needs us isn't our Church neighbor but is, like, our actual neighbor—the one who never mows her lawn and lets her dog poop on your sidewalk. Or the neighbor who's pro-choice and has a Planned Parenthood sticker on the back of her car. Or the neighbor who smokes pot that you can smell wafting up from downstairs. Or the neighbor who yells at her kids in a way you wouldn't dream of doing. These neighbors are the ones who need our love.

Jesus said a lot of stuff when he was walking around on earth. He told us to choose the better things (see Luke 10:42), to pray for our enemies (see Matthew 5:44), and to care for the poor (see Matthew 19:21). He warned us against blaspheming the Holy Spirit (see Mark 3:29) and making his Father's house a marketplace (see John 2:16). But when someone asked him what was most important, he didn't shrug and say, "Eh, I mean, it's all good." He was very clear.

The most important thing is to love God.

And the second most important thing is to love your neighbor (see Matthew 22:36–40).

I don't write this as an admonishment. It's more of my own public confession.

Let's be real: it's much, *much* easier to love a perfect, almighty God than it is to love your neighbors. Jesus is "the way and the truth and the life" (Jn 14:6). He loves you unconditionally and what he says is good.

What your nemesis says doesn't feel like the way, the truth, *or* the life. It's just annoying.

I once spoke with the head of a local pro-life group who was having a difficult time joining forces with another local pro-life group. During a collaboration meeting where things were getting tense, one member asked what exactly was dividing them. The answer could have been a thousand things: disagreements about appropriations of resources, opposing beliefs in the morality of birth control, varying levels of readiness to compromise. But what someone cautiously, carefully responded with was "Satan."

And ain't *that* the damn truth.

Satan divides us. Other people aren't your enemies. The CEO of Planned Parenthood, the loudmouth on Facebook who continuously insists that we live in a post-racial world, the people who mock "social justice warriors" while simultaneously saying that real Catholic women wear chapel veils—they're my beloved brothers and sisters. I have one enemy, and the only way to defeat him is to love.

I can roll with the questioning Christians quite easily. Women who think Catholics are too in line with the patriarchy and follow too many rules—I can understand and relate to them. When I was a missionary, the girls I was most drawn to were the questioners. Girls with blue hair and Gloria Steinem laptop stickers who said things such as, "God just doesn't want me to sit in a church building for an hour every Sunday"—I clicked with them. I don't swallow truths easily and I tend to flock to women who don't either.

The girls I have a hard time loving are those who are adamant about their rules and standards. If I had been around in Jesus' time, when he was flipping out at the Pharisees, I probably would have been standing behind him muttering "Mmm hmm" before I realized that I, too, thought I had it all figured out. I would be tsk-tsking that older brother in the prodigal son story before realizing that I was him.

Catholic feminists believe in uplifting other women, even those who make us want to roll our eyes. We can't love only people who agree with us, although wouldn't that be nice? We have to love the people who don't agree with us too.

But what does loving our neighbors look like?

To start with, I think we need to think about who our *neighbors* actually are.

I'm an advocate for thinking globally. How we eat, what we wear, what we click on—these kinds of decisions impact women across the world. We don't get to not care about women in India because we're too tired. *Everyone* is our neighbor, even if they live on the other side of the world. Like we learn in the parable of the good Samaritan (see Luke 10:25–37), just because someone isn't from our community or doesn't believe what we do doesn't mean they aren't worthy of neighborly love. And just because someone *is* a member of our community doesn't mean they're always a good neighbor. We have to think of all types of people, not just ones who look like us or live in our zip code.

But at the same time, we shouldn't forget about the women in our very own communities. Think of the women you interact with every single day: the woman who watches your kids, the woman who vacuums your apartment building hallway, the woman who makes your latte, the woman who takes her dog out at the same time you do.

Do you even know their names?

Knowing and loving the people you're surrounded by is the first step to loving your neighbor. We've had Sam Vosters on the podcast before discussing her work with Riverwest Food Pantry, a nonprofit in Milwaukee that serves the poor. Sam and the interns who work at the food pantry don't just talk the talk. They don't just give lip service by chastising rich people or tweeting about policy decisions. They literally live in the neighborhood and break bread with those they serve. They get to *know* people. They help them move, prepare for job interviews, and navigate the city. They actually love their actual neighbors. It's easy for me to daydream about packing up everything and going across the world to white-savior my way into a third world country and love on people. But if I honestly wanted to love my neighbors, maybe I should love the city of Brookfield, Wisconsin, first.

That's why my husband and I decided to dig deep into our own parish community: getting to know people is the first step toward loving them. I started attending a playgroup for moms where I was able to jump on meal trains for mamas who'd recently given birth. We actively try to chat with the people around us after Mass in order to forge new friendships. We stay in touch with our Baptism prep couple, who got us plugged into a community that regularly gets together for dinner, life-giving conversation, and intentional prayer. Between me having grown up in a city (Madison's not exactly a metropolis, but whatever) and Krzysztof having grown up moving around a lot (including across an ocean), we didn't have a firm grasp on small-town life. Few things make me feel as rooted as running into someone I know at the local coffee shop or grocery store. Before you can love people you have to know who they are. No one's going to confess the hard time they're going through to a stranger. No one's going to ask a stranger for childcare help when they encounter a sudden death in the family. But by rooting ourselves in our community, we've been able to do these things for our literal neighbors. Getting to know the people around you is a tangible way to live out the Gospel.

I think we like the idea of loving our neighbor, but like so many other things, the sacrifice scares us off. Love has to contain a sacrifice, doesn't it? Otherwise we're like the people Jesus warned us about, loving the people it's easy to love and doing the things that are easy to do (see Luke 6:32). It doesn't take much sacrifice to post a think piece about how undervalued mothers are in our society. It takes a *lot* of sacrifice to offer to watch your friend's kid on your rare day off as an emergency room nurse, as my friend Marissa did last week. One of those actions actually provides support and love to our neighbor-mothers. One gives you a buzz of "I'm awesome" energy. We must understand the difference.

If you're feeling fired up about immigration, calling your legislator or dropping off a box of baby toys to Catholic Charities is going to have a larger effect on the world than just angrily tweeting. If you want to help your best friend grow closer to Christ, having a one-on-one conversation with her about her understanding of the meaning of life will take you much further than talking to your other friends about how "lost" she is. Loving your neighbor involves treating them as Christ would—sacrificing for and serving them. Whether your neighbor is your cousin or a complete stranger, an illegal immigrant or the head of the PTA, your actual neighbor or on the other side of the world, loving your neighbor means seeing them as made in the image of God and caring about their soul and salvation. These simple principles will look differently depending on the situation but loving always comes back to remembering that your neighbor is a person made by God.

If we're ever confused about how to love someone, we just have to look at Jesus. Jesus spoke to people with kindness. He prayed for them. He corrected them, but in a gentle way. He sacrificed for them. He introduced them to the Father. These are all ways to love our neighbors.

Here is what loving your neighbor *doesn't* look like:

Assuming people have terrible intentions. These days we're very, very quick to assume our neighbor's intentions. Who someone voted for is easily translated into *Oh, so you hate women* or *Oh, so you hate Christians* or *Oh, so you hate truth and light and goodness and puppies and are basically Satan's handmaid.* Someone suggesting a slight change of liturgy at Mass means they think your parish is a totally unorthodox hot mess. Someone honestly seeking and questioning a Church teaching probably means they hate the Church, the priesthood, and you.

Assuming your neighbor has good intentions isn't a hard thing to do. Walking around with a cynical worldview, certain that everyone around you is trying to drag you down and then rolling around in your own self-righteousness, isn't holy.

So how do we *not* do this? By viewing people as God does: beautiful and broken. Whenever someone's saying something you disagree with, try to assume that they aren't a total jerk but are maybe just misguided or have different life experiences than you do that have led them to very different conclusions. Try to converse with them in a calm, collected way and see if you can find a middle ground.

Putting people into boxes. Are you a Benedict or a Francis? This question could summarize so many of our unnecessary beefs we have with one another. We long to put our Catholic sisters in boxes because then the world becomes simple and easy to understand. Wouldn't that be lovely? Wouldn't that be awesome, to know that someone's a stay-at-home mom and instantly know everything there is to know about her because all stay-at-home moms think the same? Life would be so much simpler. But alas, God made humans complex. I refuse to subscribe to the lie that people live on a binary assessment but instead insist on diving into the lion's den with Daniel (see Daniel 6)—doing the tough, scary thing, when what's comfortable seems so much safer. Getting to know someone different than you is one of the boldest actions you can take in today's society. Be the person who's willing to try to understand someone on the other side of the aisle (or pew).

Thinking that because a person's life is different than yours, they're less holy or beloved. Women make different choices. News flash—this is a good thing. God has called us all to different paths, and yours isn't the only way to heaven. You're allowed to disagree with someone's decisions and still love them unconditionally. Actually, you're *supposed* to do that. When you encounter someone who has made different choices than you and is experiencing problems, you shouldn't judge their past choices. That's not your job, sister. It's above your paygrade.

Jesus gives us our job—it's to love (see Matthew 22:36–40). It's as simple and as complicated as that. You don't get to not love people because they made different choices than you, they don't subscribe to your belief system, or they don't go to church.

Jesus didn't say, "Love your neighbor, *unless* they're kind of a hot mess."

Correcting or critiquing people with no relationship or charity. If I hear one more woman claiming that "admonish the sinner" was Jesus' number one request, I'm going to scream so hard the pearls she's clutching will fall right off. If you've never actually spoken to someone, I'm going to guess that your individualized advice isn't going to be that helpful, which only makes you a clanging cymbal. Calling someone out on their bullshit requires a relationship built on love. If you feel that your dear friend or sister needs to rethink some things in her life, and you genuinely and deeply care about her, and your greatest desire for her is to see her in heaven, and you have spent time fostering a relationship with her, I'll give you some wiggle room to critique. If you saw a girl downtown who clearly had a bit too much to drink and you loudly, audibly sighed before going home and posting on Facebook about it, you're just a jerk.

"Admonishing sinners *is* loving them," someone once said to me when I was a missionary. I probably nodded. But judgment, eye-rolling, holding up a high bar and demanding people hit it before they're worthy of your time or respect—these don't look like love to me.

Real, loving, authentic corrections need to come from a place of love. Here's Claire's Quick Guide to Whether or Not You Can Correct Someone:

1. Do you have their number in your phone?
2. Do you know them really well? (Do you know their middle name?)
3. Are they in a stable emotional place instead of a crappy hole where shit has recently hit the fan and they might burst into tears?
4. Is your honest goal to bring them closer to heaven?

5. Have you taken the log out of your own eye first? Meaning, have you made sure you're not correcting someone else for doing something that you're doing too?

If the answer to any of those questions is no, then the time isn't ripe for a sisterly correction. When I was a missionary, I had a friend who was told to go tell a girl at an event that her skirt was too short. She was like, "No. *N-O*. Not happening." And rightfully so. Could you *imagine* how that would have gone down? "Hi, person I've never met before who's taken a chance and come to a church event even though you're a college student who could be out studying or taking tequila shots. Did you know I can see two solid inches of your thigh and our Lord and Savior Jesus doesn't approve?" That girl might have seen Catholics as the world's worst humans for the rest of her life. That's not love—not even close.

Jean Valjean sings at the end of *Les Miserables* that "to love another person is to see the face of God."[1]

Just love your neighbor—the one next door and the one across the globe. It's so back-breakingly hard, and at the same time it's the easiest thing in the world.

nine

Loving Yourself

Look in the mirror. Lean in close. Don't worry; nobody's going to walk in.

What do you see?

Here's what I see when I look in the mirror: A girl in her mid-twenties who, to be honest, isn't that pretty by our cultural standards. I'm so tall that many mirrors cut off the top of my head. My hair is blonde, but not a pretty Reese Witherspoon–type blonde; it's more what they aptly call "dirty dishwater blonde." I have dark blue eyes that are really big, which sounds promising but actually tends to give off a bit-too-intense vibe. I've birthed two children so let's just say some parts of my body don't look like they did when I was in college. (Yes, I know there are many #fitspo moms out there with six-pack abs, but I'm not one of them.)

I have pretty good eyebrows, though.

The world likes to take women and critique them. Entire television shows are dedicated to weight loss and beauty competitions. I used to be completely addicted to *America's Next Top Model*, and I'll never forget watching those teeny-tiny women clomp down a runway, fighting to be the prettiest. We don't poke, prod, and measure men the way we do women. We don't put their genetics into a contest machine and hope it spits out *winner*.

But what *could* I win? I can't sing or dance. I still draw stick people. My height is incredibly deceptive, but I'll have you know

I lost the FOCUS staff training volleyball tournament for my team during my second year of training because I couldn't hit a ball that came right at me. I'm smart, but not, like, Harvard level. My kids don't get sandwiches cut into the shape of dinosaurs. I think I've already demonstrated that I'm not the holiest.

I always knew, though, that I had the hustle.

Goals. That was where I could thrive, and I learned that early on. To-do lists and office supplies? Those are my jam. Give me a goal to meet and I'll stay up until 2:00 a.m. getting there. Why I got decent grades had very little to do with natural brainpower and a lot more to do with the fact that if a door is locked I'll simply bulldoze through it. Hard work became my greatest asset. I couldn't beat anyone in a volleyball game but I could outwork them, no problem. My spreadsheets would whoop their spreadsheets' butts.

I was one of four children. That's a small family by many Catholic standards, but it sure doesn't feel small when you have three siblings. It feels loud, and at times it feels as if you have to shriek to be heard. Mucking your way through high school, college, and the business world, trying to carve a path and feeling like a blip on the screen—that feeling is hard to get away from. And although I'm incredibly blessed to come from a family that loves deeply and urgently, I view the world through a lens of accomplishments and that's a burden.

So for a long time, when I looked in the mirror I saw a girl with ambition. This isn't bad. I saw a girl who got things done, who you could depend on; a girl who could handle anything the world threw at her as long as her ponytail was tight and her coffee was strong.

The day I realized that is a pile of bullshit was a very hard day.

When I launched the podcast, it took off fairly quickly. I suddenly had an overflowing in-box, sponsors to pitch, and interviews to conduct. Throw all of that on top of my already bursting-at-the-seams day job of creating content for businesses, caring for my one-year-old, and my part-time gig as a wedding writer, and I was starting to crumble. When my husband and I were blessed with another pregnancy and I quickly realized that it was going to be round two of Barf City, I practically had a panic attack. I could barely function, and my husband was quickly burning through his vacation days.

Then there were the constant whispers in my head from Satan: *Why are you complaining? Are you kidding me? You live in a nice neighborhood in a nice state in a nice country with piles of family around you. You got pregnant on your first try with both children and spaced them a perfect two years apart. You don't have cancer. You don't even have a cold. You're not "keeping it real" by telling stories about your baby; you're slapping women with real problems in the face. You're pathetic.*

When I was a FOCUS missionary at Mizzou, a priest giving a talk on an Awakenings retreat said something that has stuck with me for years: "Both the devil and the Holy Spirit will say 'you should be holy.'"

What I thought was the Holy Spirit was far from it. The Holy Spirit whispers kindly, the devil slaps you in the face. The Holy Spirit encourages; the devil nags. If you think the same good, good father who welcomed back the prodigal son would say something like "you're pathetic," I disagree with your interpretation of scripture.

Our culture is swimming in a lack of self-love. This in and of itself is a huge problem. We don't see ourselves as being made in the image of God; we see ourselves as wildly short of perfection. I'm thoroughly convinced that even the people we know with the largest egos are overcompensating. They brag because they're trying to convince themselves of something. They compete because they're desperate for worldly approval.

God doesn't hand us worldly approval on a sparkly platter. He doesn't reward hustle with head pats.

Even as a FOCUS missionary I was determined to be the best possible missionary and earn approval through my accomplishments. I wanted to be seen as a go-getter for Jesus, as an evangelization wizard. I became obsessed with how many girls I could get into Bible study and how many I could get into discipleship, as if these kinds of things were a measure of a successful ministry. My whole life, the harder I worked, the better results I saw. I couldn't comprehend that the same approach wouldn't translate into ministry. If a girl quit Bible study, I would flip out hysterically to my poor team director, who had to gently remind me over and over again that it's *Jesus* who invites people into relationships. The fact that a girl was too busy for Wednesday Bible study *probably* didn't mean I had somehow accidently damned her to hell with my words.

But I did everything right, I wanted to yell. *I followed all the steps. I did it perfectly. I swear.*

I mean, good Lord, did I think highly of myself. It's so embarrassing to think about it now, and it's so odd how easily we can identify these flaws in others. When one of my girls in discipleship would dejectedly tell me she had tried to share the Gospel and had been shot down, I knew the truth: this girl was brave, bold, and beautiful, and she could follow steps A to Z and sometimes it just doesn't click and that had nothing to do with her. This girl came up short and, to me, there was absolutely no negative reflection on her! But when it came to *myself*, I had huge blinders on.

So now I look in the mirror and here is what I see: Yes, a dirty dishwater blonde who towers over six feet. But also a girl who tries really, really hard and messes up a lot. A girl who will go to the end of the earth for her friends and family. A girl with a short temper who cusses more than she should. A girl with a messy bun and quite a bit of mascara. A girl who tries. A girl who fails. A girl who gets back up.

A daughter of God.

We're made as daughters of God, and we should live in that knowledge. When you love yourself and truly know your worth, you're so much better able to help the world around you. To refuse to love yourself as a part of creation is to doubt the Creator.

Humility is a virtue. We're told this over and over again, and it's so true. But I think we've taken humility and warped it a bit, haven't we? It can be confusing to understand how to love yourself when you think the meaning of humility is to think you're a piece of crap. When we create something beautiful and someone compliments it, we've been conditioned to blush and shake our heads.

"No," we want to say. "It's not so good."

That's not humility.

I want to offer two alternative definitions of humility that have brought me quite a bit of peace.

The first is that humility isn't thinking less of ourselves, it's *thinking of ourselves less*. I interpret that as seeing everything I have as a gift, including any skills I may possess. And instead of thinking about how those skills can make me money or make me successful by worldly standards, I should be thinking about how they can glorify God and serve others. St. Teresa of Avila said that "true *humility* consists in being content with all that God is pleased to ordain for us, believing ourselves unworthy to be called his servants."[1]

The second is that humility is to acknowledge what is true. So are you a good singer? Praise be to God for that gift! It may be true. But what else is true? That you didn't *earn* your talent, even if you've put in hours of hard work. You may have refined it but it's God-given at the end of the day. Also, you're probably not the *best* singer in the history of the world, and you always have room to grow. (Unless your name is Beyoncé, in which case . . . hey, girl, call me.)

So I feel comfortable simultaneously saying we're in a crisis of self-love and a crisis of humility. Those two things can coexist. In fact, they *must* coexist. If we don't know who the heck we are, we can't truly love ourselves. If we see a version of ourselves that isn't complete, authentic self-love is impossible. If I only saw myself as the go-getter, incapable of failing, I don't know myself. I can't love who I don't *know*.

And so we don't think we're worth loving partners or high-paying promotions. We fear being seen as too catty or bold. We let the world tell us what women are instead of confidently knowing it in our hearts. We listen to social media and blog posts instead of the scriptures.

As women we have a unique capacity and capability for love. We can kill it for our clients and turn and weep for orphans. We can haul a screaming toddler around Target and somehow find it in us to birth another baby. Our ability to be in relationship with those around us is precious and sacred. Our gifts of love are deep within us, given by Christ. To cover them up because we're waiting for someone to give us permission is unthinkable. To restrain our moxie with the chains of a fear-based faith is a tragedy.

So how do we begin to love ourselves? I think the first step is to understand who we are.

Imagine if all women fully understood that we're powerful daughters of a King, capable of all God asks of us, be it large or small, with his kind and steady guidance. That we can save lives. That we can, as cliché as it sounds, change the world. Imagine if we didn't spend a single second of the day wondering if we were loved or cherished but instead rested in the knowledge that we *are*. Catholic women would become the truest friends, the most trusted allies, and the most powerful warriors.

If God is the source of all truth and he decides we're worthy of love, who are we to disagree? How dare we look at his creation and call it a disgrace?

Loving ourselves is some of the hardest work we'll ever do. It's not really something I can explain how to do, although I wish it were as easy as a "Ten Ways to Love Yourself" listicle or a self-help guide I could hand you in a bookstore. The truth is, it's a destination on which you never quite reach the summit. But here are some things, sister to sister, that I've found helpful.

To start with, don't say anything disparaging to yourself that you wouldn't say to a friend. I would never tell a friend that she's worthless, ugly, or weak, so why would I think those things about myself? We can't stop thoughts from popping into our heads, but we *can* stop negative self-talk in its tracks. Something as small as saying the name of Jesus out loud or making the Sign of the Cross can help me banish bad thoughts about myself and burn self-hatred into ashes. Of course, we should be examining our conscience and trying to identify areas for growth. But what holiness says is, *I struggle with the sin of gossip, and I failed today, but with the grace of God I can do better.* What self-hatred says is, *I gossiped today. I'm going to hell. I'm a terrible friend and I totally suck. Just hand me one of those headdress things and call me a Pharisee.*

Which brings me to my next point: accepting God's rich and never-ending mercy is a vital tenent of our faith. Going over our flaws with a fine-tooth comb instead of rejoicing in a God who loves us despite our imperfections is a terrible idea. By thinking that we can simply muscle our way to perfection, we're basically saying, "God, I don't need you. Thanks for the forgiveness and grace, but I'm sure if I try hard enough, I'll be just fine." But by admitting that without God we're hopeless, we're saying, "Yes, God. I want you. I love you. I need you."

I don't want you to have to spend years thinking love is something that's earned through hard work. The thought of any of you believing if you just try a little harder, you will be loved makes me want to weep. You are loved—right now, where you're sitting, whatever you're doing. Pregnant, pissed off, or presumptuous, so far from perfect, you're loved *as you are, this very minute.* You may not always *feel* it, but you need to know it.

The world is a hot mess. I'm not sure there's any political interest group who thinks we're headed in a great direction. Every time you turn on the news, you could weep at the horrors of mass shootings, child neglect, nuclear threats, and another reality star getting a divorce. So many people have different suggestions for what would make it better, whether it be new laws or new customs. But I think what the world really needs is for us to know who we are.

But we don't, so we stumble along in the dark, our heads and hearts littered with absurd half-truths and misunderstandings. We're offended and easily shaken. We fear mean looks and eye rolls. We would rather risk someone never knowing Jesus than saying hi to a stranger because we don't want to look like weirdos.

We don't know who we are, plain and simple. We don't know the truth. We don't know love and we don't know humility.

Listen, sister, because this part's important. Put down the highlighter. Shut the notebook. Refill your coffee mug, or wine glass, if that's your jam. And lean in close.

Blessed is she who has believed that the Lord would fulfill his promises to her (Lk 1:45).

His promises to fight for us (see Exodus 14:14), his promises to give power to the weak (see Isaiah 40:29), his promise to fill us with wisdom (see James 1:5), his promise to simply *be with us* (see Deuteronomy 31:8)? He'll fulfill those promises.

You're blessed beyond measure, sister. And not in a #blessed type of way, like you snagged a great parking spot, happened to grab a snapshot of your kids in their perfectly matching get-ups, or aced your final. I mean *blessed* because of the very fact of your existence as a daughter of God. Blessed be the meek and mild, but also the movers and shakers, the ones with moxie, grace, and gumption. The mamas rocking their babies back to sleep at 2:00 a.m. and the girls studying in the library at the crack of dawn. The ones folding laundry and calling their representatives and saying their Rosaries and making frappuccinos and braving the car pool line. Blessed be the poor in spirit, the feisty in spirit, and the calm in spirit. Blessed be those of us who are braving another day of snow, slush, and springtime colds. Blessed be pencil skirts and yoga pants. Blessed be women, all of you.

Conclusion

I'm very conscious of adding to the "noise."

We live in such a noisy world, it's almost cliché to point that out at this point. Twenty-four-hour news cycles, push notifications, texts, emails, and DMs fill up our phones to the point where we almost wish they would break. Everyone has a platform if they want one, whether it be a blog, podcast, or highly curated Instagram feed. Everyone can put their voice out there, and many of us choose to. It all adds up to quite a bit of noise.

I never want to be just a parrot of something someone else said better. With almost every single podcast episode, I'm thinking: Do we *need* this particular conversation? Has it happened a thousand times before? What's new about it? What do people come to *The Catholic Feminist* for that they aren't getting anywhere else?

Sometimes I don't know the answers to those questions. I start to think that every single thing that ever needs to be said has already been written in a witty think piece and shared by our cult-like news website of choice.

Do people really need to hear this?

Do people really not understand this, or do they get it by now?

Am I making a difference, or am I just giving yet another pep talk to upper-middle-class white women living in the wealthiest country in the world?

And then I hear things.

I see internet comments that tell us we're intellectually inferior and that's why Jesus didn't choose women to be disciples.

I hear a story of a woman being raped and Catholics saying she shouldn't have gotten into a car with a man in the first place.

I talk to moms who are shamed for not using their college degrees and choosing to stay home with their kids instead.

I read blog posts about how traumatizing it is for young kids when their mothers dare to pursue their passions in the career field instead of cutting their peanut butter and jelly sandwiches into hearts and stars.

I'm told that women should never be in charge of men in a work setting because it isn't biblical.

I get an Instagram comment comparing postpartum depression to a man being overly dramatic about having a cold.

I'm asked why women should feel the need to work if they have husbands who can support them.

I'm told stories about women who are asked to leave church events because their dresses are a touch on the short side.

I witness conversations questioning how Catholic a woman can truly be if she wears leggings to Mass.

I'm reminded that there are more slaves right now than at any other time in history, many of them female sex slaves.

I'm told to #shoutmyabortion, when abortion eliminates thousands of babies every year.

I'm reminded again and again that the equality of the dignity and worth of men and women is so often belittled and shoved into a box.

So, yes, we still need Catholic feminism.

And yes, sister, we still need you and your voice. We're not adding to the noise.

Now that you understand that faith and feminism can and should be blended together, you have a hefty responsibility to go out and change the world. That may sound trite, but it's true. She who knows is responsible. If you didn't want to be responsible for ending systematic racism, sex slavery, and gender stereotypes, I'm sorry if this burdens you, but . . . you are.

When the risen Jesus returned to the disciples, he knew he couldn't stay. So while he was here, he gave a great commissioning. At the end of Matthew, he implores us to raise up disciples for his Church. We're told that he is with us always, until the end of the age (see Matthew 28:18–20). So the fear and anxiety you feel should have no place in your heart. If God is for us, who can possibly be against us? The alt-right? Planned Parenthood? That annoying TA for your gender studies class? What are those in the face of Jesus Christ? What is that hurtful email in the face of all you know to be true?

I said at the beginning of this book that being a Catholic feminist raises a lot of eyebrows, but listen to me, sister: *I don't care*. I don't. The freedom I feel in Jesus is so immensely powerful, it frees me from every kind of care and concern.

Because if I say the wrong thing, Jesus forgives. His power can overcome even the stupidest of missteps. If I make a mistake, it's drowned in his grace. If I shout his words, he magnifies them. So I don't care if you say I can't be a feminist or I'm not a real Catholic. I honestly, truly, deeply don't.

I'm not saying to charge forward with a heart full of ignorance. Pick an area to which you feel most drawn. Maybe your heart beats for international orphan care, empowering modern-day mamas, or shopping ethically. If you're in college, maybe you want to take a class on social work and look into becoming a domestic violence counselor. If you're about to retire, maybe you want to research various volunteer opportunities in your local community. The world is chock-full of educational resources—just heading out to love on people probably isn't your best strategy. Study the Bible instead of buying a bumper sticker. Be strategic. Perhaps start by thinking, *What does my family need most from me right now? What about my community?* It can be as small as starting to shop more ethically when it comes to your kids' wardrobes. It can be as large as starting a nonprofit.

But you, sister, have the ability to make a difference. I don't care how rah-rah self-help kumbaya that sounds. It's true. I would hate for you to live a life of fear only to get to heaven and have Jesus sadly tell you all the good you could have done if you had trusted.

Because *what if?* What if we all lived out our faith as radically as people who actually believe that Jesus died and rose from the dead *should?* What would the world look like if we were all passionately Catholic feminists? We would be running homeless shelters and soup kitchens, combating racism and ableism, speaking up and singing loudly and leaving shame out of the whole equation. We would be receiving the Eucharist and confessing; we would be praying, opening our hearts, and raising our hands in blessing. Catholics would be the go-to people for a crisis of the heart, body, or spirit, and right now, *we're not.* But what if we were? What if when someone heard you are *Catholic,* they thought of a woman fiercely in tune with the Spirit and her neighbors, who put others before herself constantly and crushed Satan with her bare heel? What if?

Christ isn't strolling around the hallways of the office. You are.

And so I, like Jesus, want to give you a mission. Go. Learn. Seek. Do. Get off Twitter. Fill your thermos with some tea, breathe in some fresh air, and then go into the world. You have the power of Christ behind you, within you, and before you. Be not afraid, as he said.

I leave you with some words from Pope John Paul II's *Letter to Women:*

> Thank you, *women who are wives!* You irrevocably join your future to that of your husbands, in a relationship of mutual giving, at the service of love and life.
>
> Thank you, *women who are daughters* and *women who are sisters!* Into the heart of the family, and then

of all society, you bring the richness of your sensitivity, your intuitiveness, your generosity and fidelity.

Thank you, *women who work!* You are present and active in every area of life—social, economic, cultural, artistic and political. In this way you make an indispensable contribution to the growth of a culture which unites reason and feeling, to a model of life ever open to the sense of "mystery," to the establishment of economic and political structures ever more worthy of humanity.

Thank you, *consecrated women!* Following the example of the greatest of women, the Mother of Jesus Christ, the Incarnate Word, you open yourselves with obedience and fidelity to the gift of God's love. You help the Church and all mankind to experience a "spousal" relationship to God, one which magnificently expresses the fellowship which God wishes to establish with his creatures.

Thank you, *every woman,* for the simple fact of being *a woman!* Through the insight which is so much a part of your womanhood you enrich the world's understanding and help to make human relations more honest and authentic.[1]

Thank you.
Peace be with you.

Acknowledgments

They say it takes a village to raise a child. It also takes a village to make a girl a Catholic feminist and to help that girl write a book.

Thank you, thank you, thank you to the thousands of women who tune in to the show every week. I would not be living my dream life without you and your headphones. Thank you for showing up and being seen and asking the tough questions. You matter. And thank you to every single guest who has shared their story.

Heidi Hess Saxton originally reached out to me with the idea for a book, and I'm so grateful to her for taking a chance on an unpublished writer with nothing but a microphone. Amber Elder took the idea and ran with it, helping me turn a pile of words into something I'm proud of. Heidi, Amber, and the team at Ave Maria Press are amazing.

Throughout my life I've had a few friends make a deep, lasting, essential impact on my faith life. I wouldn't be the Christian I am today without Madeline Gibson, Kristin Priesler, or Levi Rash.

I'm also blessed beyond belief to have friends who will wonder and question with me without judgment, and they've watered the seeds of a messy faith life as well. So thank you to Michelle Gionet, Emily Schaefer, Jenny Parulski, Terri Meyerhofer, Marissa Mullins, and many others.

Thank you to my FOCUS teammates and all of the girls I attempted to lead at Tulane and Mizzou, especially Molly Graf and Alyssa Strickland.

A big ol' bear hug to the faith community of St. Dominic in Brookfield, Wisconsin, for giving my family the sacraments and never once rolling their eyes at my misbehaving children.

The Catholic Feminist podcast would never have been created without Pat Flynn's extensive podcasting resources.

Thank you, Peg Seiler, for the wisdom, inspirational faith, and gut-busting laughter.

Thank you to my siblings (by birth and marriage) for the sheer laughter and light you bring me: Paul Courchane, John Courchane, Jenna Courchane, Ellen Courchane, and Asia Swinarski. You can't choose your family, but if you could, I'd choose you losers anyway. To the entire Uselman/Courchane/Swinarski clans: I wouldn't be me without you.

My dad, Mark Courchane, is the smartest person I know. My mom, Grace Courchane, always knew I could do it. For those and many other reasons, I am eternally grateful and stupidly lucky. Thank you to Louise Uselman, whom I miss every single day, for raising the mama that made me a feminist.

To Benjamin and Tess, my crazy babies. You will never comprehend the joy you bring my soul.

And lastly, to Krzys. I did choose you. And I'd do it over and over and over again.

Notes

Introduction

1. See John Paul II, *Mulieris Dignitatem* (*On the Dignity and Vocation of Women*), August 15, 1988, http://w2.vatican.va/content/john-paul-ii/en/apost_letters/1988/documents/hf_jp-ii_apl_19880815_mulieris-dignitatem.html.

2. Fulton J. Sheen, *Life Is Worth Living* (San Francisco: Ignatius Press, 1999), 61.

1. Claiming Room at the Table

1. John Paul II, *Redemptoris Mater: On the Blessed Virgin Mary in the Life of the Pilgrim Church*, March 25, 1987, sec. 46, http://w2.vatican.va/content/john-paul-ii/en/encyclicals/documents/hf_jp-ii_enc_25031987_redemptoris-mater.html.

2. Roberto Colom et al., "Hippocampal Structure and Human Cognition: Key Role of Spatial Processing and Evidence Supporting the Efficiency Hypothesis in Females," *Intelligence* 41, no. 2 (March 2013): 129–40.

3. Edith Stein, *Essays on Women: The Collected Works of Edith Stein*, trans. Freda Mary Oben (Washington, DC: ICS Publications, 1996), 244.

4. Jennifer Ludden, "Ask for a Raise? Most Women Hesitate," *National Public Radio*, February 8, 2011, https://www.npr.org/2011/02/14/133599768/ask-for-a-raise-most-women-hesitate.

5. Maria Danilova, "Study Shows Gender Bias at an Early Age," *Boston Globe*, January 27, 2017, https://www.bostonglobe.com/news/nation/2017/01/26/study-shows-gender-bias-early-age/QqkTTbd2CYFR7TGAGjBLZL/story.html.

2. Embracing the Beauty in Boldness

1. Benedict XVI, "General Audience," February 14, 2007, http://w2.vatican.va/content/benedict-xvi/en/audiences/2007/documents/hf_ben-xvi_aud_20070214.html.

2. Sarah Bessey, *Jesus Feminist: An Invitation to Revisit the Bible's View of Women* (New York: Howard Books, 2013), 65.

3. Bessey, *Jesus Feminist*, 66.

4. Francis, *Gaudette Et Exultate*, March 19, 2018, para. 11, http://w2.vatican.va/content/francesco/en/apost_exhortations/documents/papa-francesco_esortazione-ap_20180319_gaudete-et-exsultate.html.

3. Finding Freedom in Service

1. John Paul II, *Mulieris Dignitatem*, http://w2.vatican.va/content/john-paul-ii/en/apost_letters/1988/documents/hf_jp-ii_apl_19880815_mulieris-dignitatem.html.

2. Martin Luther King Jr., *A Knock at Midnight: Inspiration from the Great Sermons of Reverend Martin Luther King, Jr.* (New York: Warner Books, 2000), 10.

3. Edward Le Joly and Jaya Chaliha, *Mother Teresa's Reaching Out in Love—Stories Told by Mother Teresa* (New York: Barnes and Noble, 2002), 122.

4. Mother Teresa, "Acceptance Speech" (speech, Nobel Peace Prize, University of Oslo, Norway, December 10, 1979), www.nobelprize.org/nobel_prizes/peace/laureates/1979/teresa-acceptance_en.html.

4. Being Called as a Leader

1. Judith Warner and Danielle Corley, "The Women's Leadership Gap," Center for American Progress, May 21, 2017, www.americanprogress.org/issues/women/reports/2017/05/21/432758/womens-leadership-gap.

2. John Paul II, "To the Legionaries of Christ and the Members of the Regnum Christi Movement," January 4, 2001, sec. 4, https://w2.vatican.va/content/john-paul-ii/en/speeches/2001/january/documents/hf_jp-ii_spe_20010104_legionari-cristo.html.

3. *St. Catherine of Siena as Seen in Her Letters*, trans. and ed. Vida D. Scudder (London: J. M. Dent and Sons, 1911), 185.

4. Francis X. Rocca, "Why Not Women Priests? The Papal Theologian Explains," *National Catholic Reporter*, February 5, 2013, www.ncronline.org/news/theology/why-not-women-priests-papal-theologian-explains.

5. John Paul II, *Letter to Women*, June 29, 1995, sec. 4, https://w2.vatican.va/content/john-paul-ii/en/letters/1995/documents/hf_jp-ii_let_29061995_women.html; Order of Carmelites: http://ocarm.org/en/content/ocarm/teresa-avila-quotes, accessed September 5, 2018.

6. Francis, *Gaudete Et Exsultate*, March 19, 2018, para. 12, http://w2.vatican.va/content/francesco/en/apost_exhortations/documents/papa-francesco_esortazione-ap_20180319_gaudete-et-exsultate.html.

5. Becoming Pro-Life and Pro-Women

1. "Induced Abortion in the United States," Guttmacher Institute, accessed May 5, 2018, www.guttmacher.org/fact-sheet/induced-abortion-united-states.

2. "Induced Abortion in the United States," Guttmacher Institute.

3. Mara Hvistendahl, *Unnatural Selection: Choosing Boys Over Girls, and the Consequences of a World Full of Men* (New York: PublicAffairs, 2011), xxi.

4. "6 September (1955): Flannery O'Connor to Betty Hester," American Reader, accessed August 23, 2018, http://theamericanreader.com/6-september-1955-flannery-oconnor.

5. Serrin M. Foster, "The Feminist Case against Abortion: The Pro-Life Roots of the Women's Movement," *America* 212, no. 2 (January 19–26, 2015), www.americamagazine.org/faith/2015/01/07/feminist-case-against-abortion-pro-life-roots-womens-movement.

6. Francis, *Gaudete et Exsultate*, para. 101, http://w2.vatican.va/content/francesco/en/apost_exhortations/documents/papa-francesco_esortazione-ap_20180319_gaudete-et-exsultate.html.

7. "The 100 Largest U.S. Charities," *Forbes*, accessed August 28, 2018, www.forbes.com/top-charities/list/2/#tab:rank.

8. David Paton, "The World's Biggest Charity," *Catholic Herald UK*, February 16, 2017, www.catholicherald.co.uk/issues/february-17th-2017/a-worldwide-force-for-good.

9. Gerard O'Connell, "Pope Francis: The Death Penalty Is Contrary to the Gospel," *America*, October 11, 2017, https://www.americamagazine.org/faith/2017/10/11/pope-francis-death-penalty-contrary-gospel.

6. Loving Jesus

1. David Wiley, "Pope Francis Warns Church Could Become 'Compassionate NGO,'" *BBC News,* March 14, 2013, www.bbc.com/news/world-europe-21793224.

2. Wiley, Pope Francis Warns Church Could Become 'Compassionate NGO.'"

3. "The Real Presence of Jesus Christ in the Sacrament of the Eucharist: Basic Questions and Answers," United States Conference of Catholic Bishops, accessed August 23, 2018, www.usccb.org/prayer-and-worship/the-mass/order-of-mass/liturgy-of-the-eucharist/the-real-presence-of-jesus-christ-in-the-sacrament-of-the-eucharist-basic-questions-and-answers.cfm.

4. Mike Schmitz, "What Is It Like to Hear Confessions?" Bulldog Catholic, accessed May 2, 2018, https://bulldogcatholic.org/what-is-it-like-to-hear-confessions.

7. Loving Your Vocation

1. Paul VI, *Humanae Vitae*, July 25, 1968, sec. 17, http://w2.vatican.va/content/paul-vi/en/encyclicals/documents/hf_p-vi_enc_25071968_humanae-vitae.html.

2. Charlotte Wessel Skovlund, "Association of Hormonal Contraception with Depression," *JAMA Psychiatry* 73, no. 11 (November 2016): 1154–62, doi:10.1001/jamapsychiatry.2016.2387.

3. Charlotte Wessel Skovlund et al., "Association of Hormonal Contraception with Suicide and Suicide Attempts," *American Journal of Psychiatry* 175, no. 4 (November 2017): 336–42, doi:10.1176/appi.ajp.2017.17060616.

4. Charlotte Wessel Skovlund et al., "Contemporary Hormonal Contraception and the Risk of Breast Cancer," *New England Journal of Medicine* 378, no. 13 (March 2018): 1265–66, doi:10.1056/NEJMoa1700732.

5. Jenny Uebbing, "When NFP Is Hard to Swallow," *Mama Needs Coffee* (blog), October 24, 2014, accessed May 2 2018, https://www.catholicnewsagency.com/mamaneedscoffee/2014/10/when-nfp-is-hard-to-swallow.

6. Edith Stein, "Ethos of Women's Professions," accessed September 6, 2018, http://www.oikonomia.it/index.php/it/49-oikonomia-2014/giugno-2014/330-ethos-of-woman-s-professions-1930.

7. Francis, *Gaudete et Exsultate*, para. 14, http://w2.vatican.va/content/francesco/en/apost_exhortations/documents/papa-francesco_esortazione-ap_20180319_gaudete-et-exsultate.html.

8. Loving Your Neighbor

1. "Valjean's Death," *Les Miserables*, directed by Tom Hooper (Universal City, CA: Universal Pictures, 2012).

9. Loving Yourself

1. Bonaventure Hammer, ed., *Mary, Help of Christians and the 14 Saints Invoked as Holy Helpers* (Whitefish, MO: Kessinger, 2008), 395.

Conclusion

1. St. John Paul II, *Letter to Women*, Libreria Editrice Vaticana, June 29, 1995, sec. 2, https://w2.vatican.va/content/john-paul-ii/en/letters/1995/documents/hf_jp-ii_let_29061995_women.html.

CLAIRE SWINARSKI is a writer who founded and hosts *The Catholic Feminist* podcast. She served as a FOCUS missionary from 2013 to 2015.

A 2013 graduate of the University of Wisconsin–Madison, she has a bachelor's degree in mass communication and political science, with a certificate in criminal justice. She has appeared on numerous podcasts, including *The Catholic Hipster*, *Catching Foxes*, *Girlfriends*, and *Jesuitical*. Her work has been featured in *Radiant* magazine, Blessed Is She, and FemCatholic. She has written for publications including the *Washington Times*, *Good Housekeeping*, *Cosmopolitan*, *Seventeen*, *Verily*, *Relevant*, and *America*.

Swinarski and her husband, Krzysztof, live with their family in Brookfield, Wisconsin.

www.thecatholicfeministpodcast.com
Facebook: thecatholicfeministpodcast
Instagram: @thecatholicfeminist